Scott Fisher
- Bachelor's Degree in History: University of Michigan
- Master's Degree in Korean Studies: Seoul National University, Korea
- Master's Degree in International Security: Georgetown University
- PhD in International Relations, pending, Rutgers University
- authored dozens of books and articles on Korean culture, 'Konglish', and language study
- former English professor at Ewha Woman's University and Sungshin Women's University
- former Korean researcher, translator, Georgetown University
- former co-host of *EBS Morning Special* and numerous other EBS radio and TV programs

Brian Stuart
- Bachelor's Degree in Mass Communications/Journalism: University of Utah
- Master's Degree in TESL: University of Birmingham, UK
- former EBS co-host for two English conversation programs
- Business English Professor at Korea Manpower Association
- Video lecturer for various Internet ESL companies
- more than 15 years teaching experience at various universities in Seoul, Korea

Authors: Scott Fisher, Brian Stuart
Publisher: Chung Kyudo
Editors: Chung Soyeon, Im Soyun
Designers: Kim Nakyung, Cho Hwayeon, Park Sunyoung
Illustrator: Park Jiho

First Published in October 2014
By Darakwon, Inc.
Darakwon Bldg., 211, Munbal-ro, Paju-si, Gyeonggi-do 10881
Republic of Korea
Tel: 82-2-736-2031 (Ext. 550)
Fax: 82-2-732-2037

Copyright © 2014 Scott Fisher, Brian Stuart

All rights reserved. No part of this publication may be reproduced, stored in a retrieval system, or transmitted in any form or by any means, electronic, mechanical, photocopying or otherwise, without the prior consent of the copyright owner. Refund after purchase is possible only according to the company regulations. Contact the above telephone number for any inquiry. Consumer damages caused by loss, damage etc. can be compensated according to consumer dispute resolution standards announced by the Korea Fair Trade Commission. An incorrectly collated book will be exchanged.

ISBN: 978-89-277-0729-5 18740
      978-89-277-0728-8 18740(set)

www.darakwon.co.kr

[Components] Student Book / Free MP3 Available Online
15 14 13 12 11 10 9   25 26 27 28 29

DARAKWON

CONTENTS

To Our Readers	6
Study Guide	7
Plan of Book 1	8

UNIT 01	Meeting People	10
UNIT 02	Everyday Life	18
UNIT 03	Asking for Directions	26
UNIT 04	Entertainment and Leisure	34
UNIT 05	Holidays and Family	42
UNIT 06	Dating	50
UNIT 07	Phones and Text Messages	58
UNIT 08	Jobs	66
UNIT 09	Food	74
UNIT 10	Shopping and Fashion	82
UNIT 11	Weather and Seasons	90
UNIT 12	Sports and Injuries	98

Appendix

- Activity File	108
- Listening Script	112
- Wrap-it-up Questions	116
- Answers	122
- Go Fish	127

To Our Readers

As the saying goes, it's amazing how time flies. It's been almost eight years since the first edition of Speaking for Everyday Life appeared on the shelves of bookstores and universities in Korea. Our initial aim in writing the two-series textbooks was to offer a specialized English-language textbook that was specifically targeted at Korean learners of English, especially at the university level. It seems that we answered a need, because both books have enjoyed popularity in marketplace. For that, we are especially grateful to all the teachers and students who have used and learned from our books.

Eight years on, it is time to overhaul and update the material in these textbooks. We hope we have accomplished this goal, while remaining true to our original intent of providing material that is specifically relevant to Korean students. The material in each unit has been examined and updated, while keeping a focus on addressing common mistakes that Korean students make when they produce English. Every conversation in the book has been rewritten in as authentic a style as possible. All the "Konglish" sections have been updated and expanded. Extra vocabulary and usage notes have also been added to the units.

We hope that teachers and students will find these changes beneficial as they pursue their respective goals in English education. For teachers, there are all new units to draw upon for both teaching in the classroom and for generating material for tests. Please remember that the original textbooks can now be used for extra test material that students may not be aware of, but which fits nicely into each new unit of the second edition. For students, we hope that the extra vocabulary, usage notes, and conversation will help you get a sense of how English is actually used by native speakers. Also, by keeping the focus on subjects that are commonly discussed by Korean students, we hope you will feel comfortable discussing these topics after studying the units.

The authors would like to extend their thanks again to the original group of colleagues who generously gave their time in proofreading and suggesting improvements: Ian Leighton, Carla Supple, Ben Jorgenson, Kevin Christman, Dan Harmon and Christian Thompson. Anything the books lack is our mistake, anything it does well is due to their generous support.

We also owe a particular debt of gratitude to the editors of Darakwon. Without the hard work and patience of the editors, these books would not be a reality.

As before, we hope that these textbooks help you create a refreshing and interesting atmosphere in your classrooms. We wish you the best of luck in achieving your goals, not only with your English studies, but in your lives as well.

Thank you,

Scott Fisher and Brian Stuart

Study Guide

Each unit starts with vocabulary and ideas that are core to that unit's theme. Two conversations and listening activities help students learn the target vocabulary and grammar. Most importantly, each unit features numerous activities for students to actually practice the language. Wrapping up each unit are 'free talking' questions designed to improve both listening and speaking.

Vocabulary
explains and practices key expressions

Conversations
build on the unit's theme by modeling key phrases and grammar

Activity
give students several chances to practice the new grammar and expressions

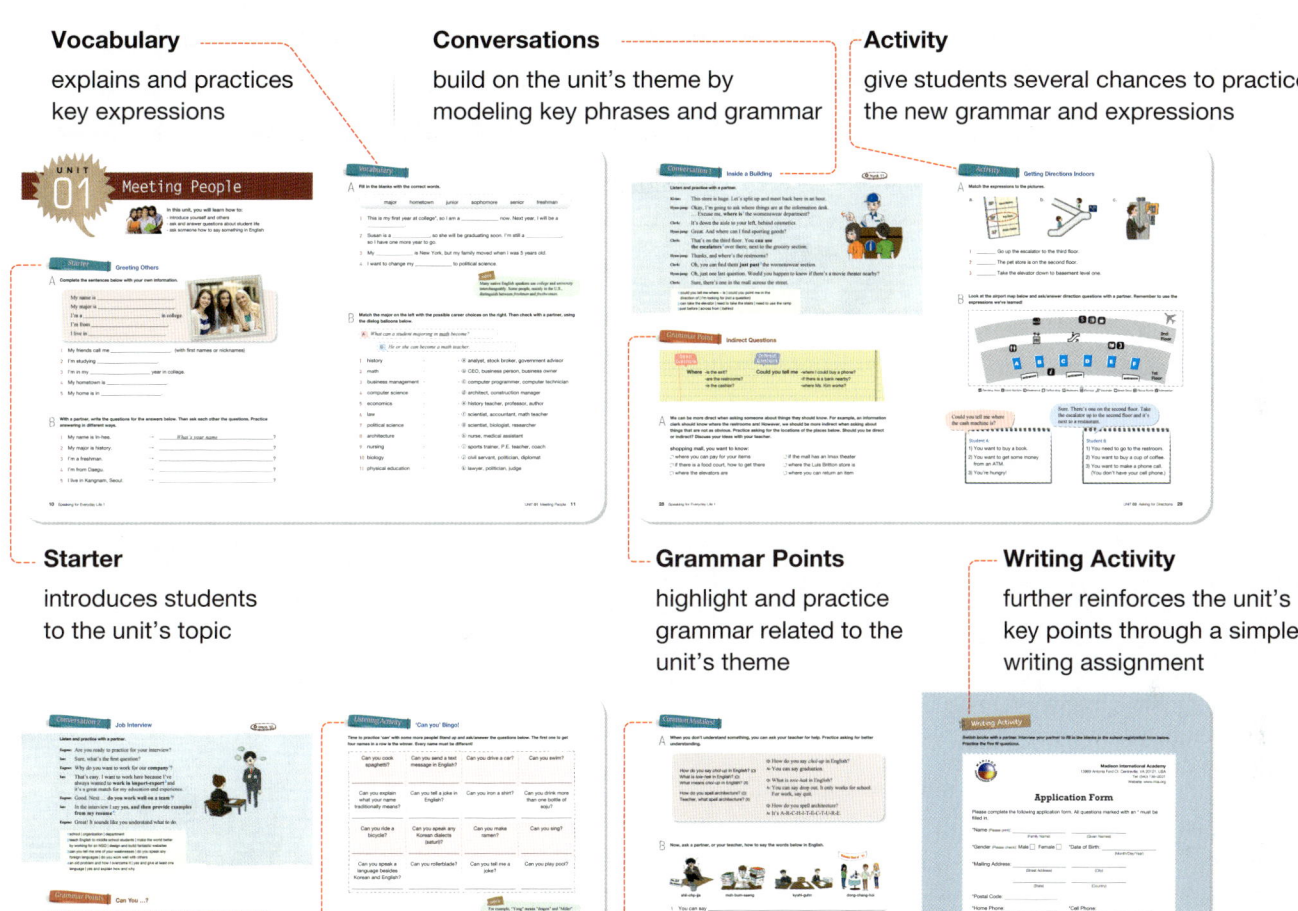

Starter
introduces students to the unit's topic

Grammar Points
highlight and practice grammar related to the unit's theme

Writing Activity
further reinforces the unit's key points through a simple writing assignment

Listening Activity
serves to review the unit's main concepts, vocabulary and grammar

Common Mistakes
clears up some problem 'Konglish' and highlights related cultural points

Wrap-it-up Questions
helps imprint the unit's key expressions and grammar through 'free talking' questions

MP3 Files Available Online
- contains the two main conversations and listening activities from each unit.

Plan of Book 1

Unit	Title	Functions	Vocabulary
Unit 01	Meeting People	• introduce yourself and others • discuss student life • ask how to say something in English	• college majors • year in college
Unit 02	Everyday Life	• tell time • use time prepositions • describe daily activities	• prepositions of time • daily activities
Unit 03	Asking for Directions	• ask for and give directions • use prepositions of place • ask indirect questions	• direction commands • prepositions of place
Unit 04	Entertainment and Leisure	• talk about hobbies and interests • invite someone to do something • accept/decline/reschedule invitations	• hobbies and interests • invitations
Unit 05	Holidays and Family	• talk about days and dates • discuss Korean holidays • use family-related expressions	• days of the week • months of the year • holidays & special days • family-related terms
Unit 06	Dating	• describe appearance • describe personality • tell stories about past events	• appearance adjectives • personality adjectives
Unit 07	Phones and Text Messages	• leave and take messages • send text messages in English	• phones and messages
Unit 08	Jobs	• how to use 'can' • common interview questions • basic résumé writing	• careers and jobs • resume expressions
Unit 09	Food	• describe food • use countable/uncountable nouns • use comparatives	• food – types and tastes • comparison adjectives
Unit 10	Shopping and Fashion	• describe clothing • use this/that/these/those • talk about prices	• clothing (fabric & style) • compliments • numbers
Unit 11	Weather and Seasons	• describe the weather • talk about the four seasons • answer 'how often' questions	• weather expressions • seasonal expressions • frequency expressions
Unit 12	Sports and Injuries	• describe various sports • invite someone to play a sport • describe injuries	• sport descriptions • injuries

Activities	Grammar	Listening	Writing
• meet classmates • introduce someone • cross-culture questions	• five 'W' questions	• common introduction phrases	• fill out a school application
• daily activities • questions about schedules • 'time' bingo	• prepositions of time • simple present tense	• match activities with times	• daily planner/ schedule
• give directions inside • give street directions	• commands • ask indirect questions	• understand directions	• create a map to your home
• discuss likes & dislikes • make/accept invitations • decline/reschedule invitations	• likes and dislikes – affirmative and negative answers • make invitations	• identify times, places & activities	• social interests questionnaire
• calendars • special days • holiday differences • discuss your family	• time prepositions – in and on	• understanding dates and times	• make a family tree
• discuss your ideal partner • be a matchmaker • talk about a date	• simple past vs. past progressive • when/while/as	• describe appearance • describe personality	• a romantic first meeting
• take a message • short phone conversations	• make polite requests/ refusals	• take a phone message • understand a phone conversation	• write English text messages
• match person to job • mini job interview • can you ... ? bingo	• 'can' questions and answers	• identify career goals	• make a résumé
• recipes • compare foods • bingo with foods & adjectives	• countable/uncountable nouns – much/many/ some/a little/a few • comparatives	• identify foods and opinions	• make comparisons
• going shopping • using different currencies • fashion show	• demonstratives – this/that/these/those/ one/it	• identify products and prices	• describe clothing important to you
• weather report • What's the weather like in...? • how often do you...?	• frequency expressions – how often...?	• understand a weather report	• fill-in-the-blank weather report
• Go Fish! • describe injuries	• superlatives	• understand opinions and frequency	• survey people

UNIT 01 Meeting People

In this unit, you will learn how to:
- introduce yourself and others
- ask and answer questions about student life
- ask someone how to say something in English

Starter   Greeting Others

A Complete the sentences below with your own information.

My name is _____.
My major is _____.
I'm a _____ in college.
I'm from _____.
I live in _____.

1 My friends call me _____. (with first names or nicknames)
2 I'm studying _____.
3 I'm in my _____ year in college.
4 My hometown is _____.
5 My home is in _____.

B With a partner, write the questions for the answers below. Then ask each other the questions. Practice answering in different ways.

1 My name is In-hee.   →   *What's your name* ?
2 My major is history.   →   _____ ?
3 I'm a freshman.   →   _____ ?
4 I'm from Daegu.   →   _____ ?
5 I live in Kangnam, Seoul. →   _____ ?

Vocabulary

A Fill in the blanks with the correct words.

> major   hometown   junior   sophomore   senior   freshman

1. This is my first year at college*, so I am a _____ now. Next year, I will be a _____.

2. Susan is a _____, so she will be graduating soon. I'm still a _____, so I have one more year to go.

3. My _____ is New York, but my family moved when I was 5 years old.

4. I want to change my _____ to political science.

NOTE: Many native English speakers use *college* and *university* interchangeably. Some people, mainly in the U.S., distinguish between *freshman* and *freshwoman*.

B Match the major on the left with the possible career choices on the right. Then check with a partner, using the dialog balloons below.

> **A** What can a student majoring in <u>math</u> become?
>
> **B** He or she can become a math teacher.

1. history
2. math
3. business management
4. computer science
5. economics
6. law
7. political science
8. architecture
9. nursing
10. biology
11. physical education

ⓐ analyst, stock broker, government advisor
ⓑ CEO, business person, business owner
ⓒ computer programmer, computer technician
ⓓ architect, construction manager
ⓔ history teacher, professor, author
ⓕ scientist, accountant, math teacher
ⓖ scientist, biologist, researcher
ⓗ nurse, medical assistant
ⓘ sports trainer, P.E. teacher, coach
ⓙ civil servant, politician, diplomat
ⓚ lawyer, politician, judge

UNIT 01 Meeting People 11

Conversation 1 — Meeting New People

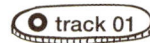

Listen and practice with a partner.

Sam: Hi, are you a computer sciences major?

Hyun-jung: Yes, how did you know that?

Sam: I saw your book. **I'm**[1] Sam, by the way.

Hyun-jung: I'm Hyun-jung. **Nice to meet you**[2]. I'm a freshman, so I don't know many people here.

Sam: Where are you from?

Hyun-jung: I'm from Korea. **How about you**[3]?

Sam: I'm from here, L.A. I want to be an architect, so **I'm studying**[4] architecture.

1 I am ~. | My friends call me ~.
2 It's nice to meet you. | Good to meet you. | Nice meeting you.
3 How about you? | What about you? | And you?
4 I'm majoring in ~. | My major is ~.

Practice — Five "W" Questions

A Complete the sentences with your own information.

1 Who is your favorite professor? → My favorite professor is _____.

2 What are you majoring in? → My major is / I'm majoring in _____.

3 Where are you from? → I'm from _____.

4 When did you start college? → I started college _____.

5 Why are you studying history? → I want to _____.

B Make questions to match the answers below.

1 My favorite professor is Dr. Kim. → _____?

2 My major is Physical Education → _____?

3 I'm from Thailand. → _____?

4 I started college last year. → _____?

5 I want to be a history teacher. → _____?

Class Activity

A Practice by getting up and walking around class, and talking to some new people. Before everyone gets up, start by asking your teacher.

NAME	WHERE FROM	MAJOR	YEAR
teacher			*Skip teacher here*

B In the box below, write down *OK* or *Not OK* depending on whether the question is acceptable or not. Some ideas may fit both cultures.

	Dating	Korea	English-speaking Countries
1	Where are you from?		
2	How old are you?		
3	Where did you go to college?		
4	What do you do?		
5	How much money do you make?		
6	Are you a Christian?		
7	Why aren't you married?		
8	Do you have any children?		
9	Why don't you have any children?		
10	How big is your family?		
11	Who will you vote for?		
12	How much do you weigh?		

NOTE
Negative questions (Why aren't you…? / Why don't you…?) often sound rude.

C Now you are ready to start asking polite questions of native English speakers. Begin with your teacher. Your teacher might ask you questions too.

Conversation 2 — Introducing Others

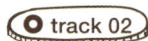

Listen and practice with a partner.

Hyun-jung: Hi Susan. I'd like you to meet Tae-il. Tae-il, this is Susan.

Susan: I'm very sorry, **how do you spell that**[1]?

Tae-il: No problem. It's T-A-E dash I-L. My friends call me "Tae".

Susan: Are you a computer science major also, Tae?

Hyun-jung: No, he's studying architecture, like you! I thought you two should meet.

Susan: Oh, that's great. What year are you in, Tae?*

Tae-il: I'm a junior. I'm taking Advanced Concepts in Architecture with Professor Christman.

Susan: Oh, **me too**[2]! We should study together!

1 could you spell that for me
2 so am I

NOTE
"What grade are you in?" is only used for elementary, middle, and high school students.

Class Activity

A Do you remember making and asking questions after the first conversation in this unit? Get into groups of four and use that information to introduce your former partner to your new ones. Take turns.

A: _____, this is _____.
_____, this is _____.
B: Nice to meet you, _____.
A: You too, _____.
A: _____ is majoring in _____.
B: He/She wants to be a _____.

Follow up ideas
What year is he/she in?
Who is his/her favorite professor?
Where is he/she from?

B Once everyone is finished, your teacher will choose a few people to perform their introductions in front of the class.

Listening Activity

A Imagine this conversation is taking place at a party. Listen and fill in the blanks.

Terry: Hi, I'm Terry.
Su-jin: Hi Terry, I'm Su-jin. _____.
Terry: Same here. Do you go to UCLA?
Su-jin: No, I'm visiting a friend here. _____ at a university in Seoul, Korea.
Terry: Oh, I'm _____ at UCLA. I'm studying _____.
Su-jin: What a coincidence! I'm studying biology too! But I'm _____.

B Now Su-jin introduces Terry to her friend, Min-jeong. Listen and check *true* or *false*.

1. Min-jeong is a junior.   True _____   False _____
2. Terry is Australian.   True _____   False _____
3. Min-jeong is studying law.   True _____   False _____
4. Su-jin and Min-jeong met in college. True _____   False _____

Pronunciation

Listen to and repeat the expressions below.

Written

My name is Kevin.
Nice to meet you.
Where are you from?
Who is your favorite professor?
Where is your school?
When is your birthday?

Spoken

My name's Kevin.
Nice'ta meet cha.
Where'ya from?
Who's your favorite professor?
Where's your school?
When's your birthday?

Common Mistakes!

A When you don't understand something, you can ask your teacher for help. Practice asking for better understanding.

How do you say *chol-up* in English? (O)
What is *toie-hak* in English? (O)
What means *chol-up* in English? (X)

How do you spell architecture? (O)
Teacher, what spell architecture? (X)

Q: How do you say *chol-up* in English?
A: You can say graduation.

Q: What is *toie-hak* in English?
A: You can say drop out. It only works for school. For work, say quit.

Q: How do you spell architecture?
A: It's A-R-C-H-I-T-E-C-T-U-R-E.

B Now, ask a partner or your teacher, how to say the words below in English.

shil-ohp-jja

moh-bum-saeng

kyuhl-guhn

dong-chang-hoi

1 You can say _____.

2 You can say _____.

3 It means _____ in English.

4 It means _____ in English.

16 Speaking for Everyday Life 1

Writing Activity

Switch books with a partner. Interview your partner to fill in the blanks in the school registration form below. Practice the five *W* questions.

Madison International Academy
13969 Antonia Ford Ct. Centreville, VA 20121, USA
Tel: (540) 736–2031
Website: www.mia.org

Application Form

Please complete the following application form. All questions marked with an * must be filled in.

*Name (Please print): _____ _____
                         (Family Name)   (Given Names)

*Gender (Please check): Male ☐ Female ☐   *Date of Birth: _____
                                                               (Month/Day/Year)

*Mailing Address: _____ _____
                    (Street Address)   (City)

                  _____ _____
                        (State)   (Country)

*Postal Code: _____

*Home Phone: _____   *Cell Phone: _____

*Citizenship: _____   *Email Address: _____

                                             _____
                                             Please sign here.

                                       *Date: _____
                                              (Month/Day/Year)

> **NOTE:** 'Print your name' and 'Sign your name' mean different things.

Wrap-it-up Questions

Get into groups of four. Turn to 'Wrap-it-up Questions' in the back of this book. Students should ONLY look at their own questions.

UNIT 02 Everyday Life

In this unit, you will learn how to:
- tell time
- use proper time prepositions
- describe your daily activities

Starter Telling Time

A With a partner, look at the pictures below and write down what happens at the times listed.

1 6:00 a.m.

I get up at six.

2 7:00 a.m.

3 7:30 a.m.

4 8:15 a.m.

5 9:00 a.m.-10:00 p.m.

6 12:00 a.m.

B With a partner, write the questions to the answers below. Then ask each other the questions.

1 I get up at 6:00. → *What time do you get up* ?
2 I take a shower at 6:30. → _____?
3 I eat breakfast at 7:00. → _____?
4 I get to school at 8:15. → _____?
5 I study from 9:00 a.m. to 10:00 p.m. → _____?
6 I go to bed at midnight. → _____?

Vocabulary

A Put the expressions in the blanks below.

> get   midnight   leave   stay up late   from … to   noon   sleep in/late

1. Twelve o'clock is special. During the day it is also called _____, but at night it is called _____.
2. I _____ home in the morning at 7:30 a.m. and _____ home at 5:00 p.m.
3. I charge my phone while I sleep, usually _____ 12:30 _____ 6:30.
4. On Friday and Saturday night I _____ because I can _____ the next morning.

> get dressed (put on clothes)   brush my teeth   put on makeup   wake up

5. _____
6. _____
7. _____
8. _____

B Write *in*, *on*, or *at* for the expressions below.

1. _____ 10:30
2. _____ Sunday
3. _____ the morning/afternoon/evening
4. _____ October
5. _____ night
6. _____ noon/midnight
7. _____ 2015
8. _____ weekends
9. _____ around 7:30

NOTE
It's also common to just say, "I'll meet you around 7:30."

C Fill out Jennifer's Saturdays with the proper prepositions. Use *before, at, on, in, from,* or *to*.

9:30 a.m.	Get up
10:00 a.m.~12:00 p.m.	Watch TV
10:30 a.m.	Eat breakfast
1:30 p.m.	Go jogging
2:30 p.m.	Eat lunch and check messages
8:00 p.m.~12:00 a.m.	Hang out with friends

1. _____ Saturdays, Jennifer gets up _____ 9:30 a.m. and watches TV _____ ten _____ noon.
2. Also _____ the morning, _____ around 10:30, she eats breakfast.
3. _____ she eats lunch, she goes jogging.
4. After jogging, _____ 2:30 p.m., she eats lunch and checks her messages.
5. She hangs out with friends _____ eight _____ midnight.

Conversation 1

Making a Lunch Date!

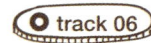

Listen and practice with a partner.

Jay: What time is it?

Sang-mi: It's quarter to ten[1]. Why?

Jay: Class starts at ten. Bye!

Sang-mi: **What time does it end[2]?**

Jay: Around noon. Get lunch after class?

Sang-mi: Sure. How about 12:30 in the cafeteria?

Jay: Great. See you then.

1 nine forty-five
2 What time is it finished/done/over/through?

Grammar Points

What Time Is It?

It's 9 o'clock.　　It's almost ten.　　It's ten to/before six.　　It's 5:15.

It's 5:30 in the morning. / It's 5:30 a.m.　　It's 5:30 in the afternoon.　　It's 11:30 in the morning.　　It's 11:30 at night. / It's 11:30 p.m.

NOTE

Konglish – I get up at a.m. seven.
English – I get up at seven a.m.

Activity — Daily Routine

A First, write down what you normally do at these times. Then share your schedule with a partner and write down your partner's schedule by listening to what your partner says and then write it down. Do NOT look at your partner's book!

> Hyun-sook, what do you usually do at 6 a.m.?
>
> I usually wake up at 6.
>
> I'm sleeping at 6. How about you?

You
- 6:00 a.m. _____
- 9:10 a.m. _____
- 10:30 a.m. _____
- 12:00 p.m. _____
- 1:45 p.m. _____
- 5:50 p.m. _____
- 11:45 p.m. _____

Partner
- 6:00 a.m. _____
- 9:10 a.m. _____
- 10:30 a.m. _____
- 12:00 p.m. _____
- 1:45 p.m. _____
- 5:50 p.m. _____
- 11:45 p.m. _____

NOTE Remember '12:00 p.m.' is also called 'noon'.

B Now, right down three questions to ask your teacher about his/her daily life. Next, ask and answer the questions with your teacher.

1. What do you usually do at _____?
2. _____
3. _____

Conversation 2 — Are You Busy Tomorrow?

 track 07

Listen and practice with a partner.

Jae-suk: Are you okay? You seem stressed.

Dong-mi: I'm taking too many classes. My weekdays are too busy.

Jae-suk: That's too bad. At least tomorrow is Saturday though, you can **sleep late**[1].

Dong-mi: I know. I sleep until 10 or 11 every **weekend**[2].

Jae-suk: Good, it sounds like you need **a break**[3]. How about after you get up, are you busy tomorrow afternoon?

Dong-mi: No, I should be free after one or two. Why?

Jae-suk: Do you want to see a movie?

Dong-mi: Sure, text me tomorrow afternoon.

1 sleep in | wake up late | get up late
2 Saturday and Sunday
3 some rest | some free time | some down time

Activity — Gap Fill

Look at the chart below. Ask and answer questions with your partner to fill in the missing information. (Student B turns to page 108.)

Student A: What does Marisa do at 7:10 a.m.?

Student B (looking at chart): She gets up at 7:10. What does she do at noon?

Student A: At noon she eats lunch. What does she do at …?

Chart for student A

Name & Routine	wake up	go to school	class	lunch
Marisa	7:40			12:00
Steve			math	
Your Partner				

22 Speaking for Everyday Life 1

Time Bingo

Stand up and ask/answer the questions below with your classmates. The first student to get five **DIFFERENT** names in a row (across, down, or diagonal) is the winner! Only write down a name if someone answers YES. If they answer no, write nothing and ask a different question or a different classmate.

Do you have a class after 6:00 p.m.?

sleep in on weekends _Tae-joon_	get up at 6 in the morning	have a part-time job in the evening	do homework in the morning	get to school before 9 a.m.
play computer games until midnight	eat breakfast before 8 a.m.	meet your boy/girlfriend on weekends	have class until 8 in the evening	hate classes in the morning
have class on weekends	go to bed around 11 at night	exercise on weekdays	skip breakfast in the morning	study everyday from Monday to Friday
surf the Internet until 2 a.m.	hate classes late at night	clean your house on weekends	ride a bus from 9 to 9:30 a.m.	take a shower in the evening
brush your teeth 3 times a day	go to church on Sunday mornings	go shopping on weekend afternoons	hang out around school after class	meet friends at lunchtime

Listening Activity

A Listen to the dialog and match the times with the activities. 🎧 track 08

11:15 p.m.   10:30 p.m.   9:40 p.m.

1 _____   2 _____   3 _____

B Listen to the dialog and answer the questions. 🎧 track 09

1 What time did the woman text the man? _____
2 What was the woman doing late at night? _____
3 What time did the man go to bed? _____
4 What time did the man wake up? _____
5 Why did the man sleep so long? _____

Common Mistakes!

Change the Konglish expressions to English ones.

1 I slept eight *times* last night.   → I slept _____ last night.
2 Class ends at *p.m. 4*.   → Class ends _____.
3 *In this weekend*, I'll study hard.   → _____, I'll study hard.
4 *During midnight*, I sleep.   → _____ midnight, I _____.
5 On weekdays, I *sleep at 11*.   → On weekdays, I _____ at 11.
6 Class starts *next week Monday*.   → Class starts _____.
7 I *wear my clothes* at 7:30.   → I _____ at 7:30.

24 Speaking for Everyday Life 1

Writing Activity

Who is the busiest person in your family? Fill in the schedules below for at least two family members. Use the expressions you've learned in this unit. You will need to interview your family members (try it in English!) to do this activity.

	You	Mom	Dad	Brother / Sister	Pet
6:00 a.m.					
8:00					
9:00					
10:30					
noon					
1:00 p.m.					
3:30					
5:00					
6:30					
8:00					
midnight					

Wrap-it-up Questions

Get into groups of four. Turn to 'Wrap-it-up Questions' in the back of the book. Only read your own questions! Listen carefully when other students ask you a question, then answer using the expressions we learned in this unit.

UNIT 03 Asking for Directions

In this unit, you will learn how to:
- ask for and give directions
- describe where things are using prepositions of place
- use indirect questions to be more polite

Starter

Asking for Directions

A Listen to three expressions used by people who want to know where things are. Rank the expressions from most polite (1) to least polite (3). Also, circle where you think the speaker is.

1   Rank _____   bank   street   supermarket
2   Rank _____   department store   airport   street
3   Rank _____   airport   countryside   supermarket

B Draw arrows to match and complete the sentences.

1   Where   ·   · could you   ·   · where the nearest   ·   · the shampoo?
2   Excuse me, ·   · happen to know   ·   · keep   ·   · where gate 57 is?
3   Would you ·   · do you   ·   · please tell me   ·   · subway station is?

C Match the landmarks with the correct letter.

1   subway station _____
2   intersection _____
3   crosswalk _____
4   foot bridge _____
5   traffic light _____
6   bus stop _____
7   taxi stand _____

26   Speaking for Everyday Life 1

Vocabulary

A Common Commands for Giving Directions

Turn right.
= Make a right turn.
= Hang a right.
> Take a right at the next intersection.
> Turn right on Main Street.

Turn left.
= Make a left turn.
= Hang a left.
> Go left at the next traffic light.
> Turn left into the alley.

Go straight.
= Keep going straight.
= Go (straight) through the intersection.
> Go up one block.*
> Go down one block.*

Cross the street.
= Go across the street.
= Use the crosswalk.
= Get on the other side of the street.

*Usually these sentences have exactly the same meaning, but if there is a hill or mountain, use the appropriate one.

B Prepositions of Place

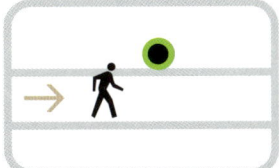

It's **on your left**.

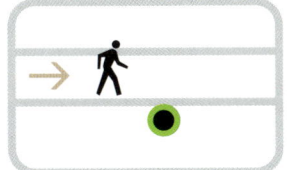

It's **on your right**.

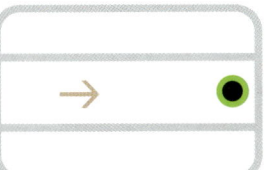

It's **straight ahead**.

It's **next to** the coffee shop.

It's **just past** the coffee shop.

It's **just before** the coffee shop.

It's **on the corner**.

It's **kitty corner to** the coffee shop.

It's **across from** the coffee shop.

UNIT 03 Asking for Directions

Conversation 1 — Inside a Building

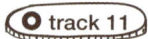

Listen and practice with a partner.

Ki-tae: This store is huge. Let's split up and meet back here in an hour.

Hyun-jung: Okay, I'm going to ask where things are at the information desk. … Excuse me, **where is**[1] the womenswear department?

Clerk: It's down the aisle to your left, behind cosmetics.

Hyun-jung: Great. And where can I find sporting goods?

Clerk: That's on the third floor. You **can use the escalators**[2] over there, next to the grocery section.

Hyun-jung: Thanks, and where's the restrooms?

Clerk: Oh, you can find them **just past**[3] the womenswear section.

Hyun-jung: Oh, just one last question. Would you happen to know if there's a movie theater nearby?

Clerk: Sure, there's one in the mall across the street.

1 could you tell me where ~ is | could you point me in the direction of | I'm looking for (not a question)
2 can take the elevator | need to take the stairs | need to use the ramp
3 just before | across from | behind

Grammar Point — Indirect Questions

Direct Questions	Indirect Questions
Where -is the exit?	**Could you tell me** -where I could buy a phone?
-are the restrooms?	-if there is a bank nearby?
-is the cashier?	-where Ms. Kim works?

A We can be more direct when asking someone about things they should know. For example, an information clerk should know where the restrooms are! However, we should be more indirect when asking about things that are not as obvious. Practice asking for the locations of the places below. Should you be direct or indirect? Discuss your ideas with your teacher.

shopping mall, you want to know:

☐ where you can pay for your items
☐ if there is a food court, how to get there
☐ where the elevators are
☐ if the mall has an Imax theater
☐ where the Luis Britton store is
☐ where you can return an item

Speaking for Everyday Life 1

Activity — Getting Directions Indoors

A Match the expressions to the pictures.

a.    b.    c.

1. _____ Go up the escalator to the third floor.
2. _____ The pet store is on the second floor.
3. _____ Take the elevator down to basement level one.

B Look at the airport map below and ask/answer direction questions with a partner. Remember to use the expressions we have learned!

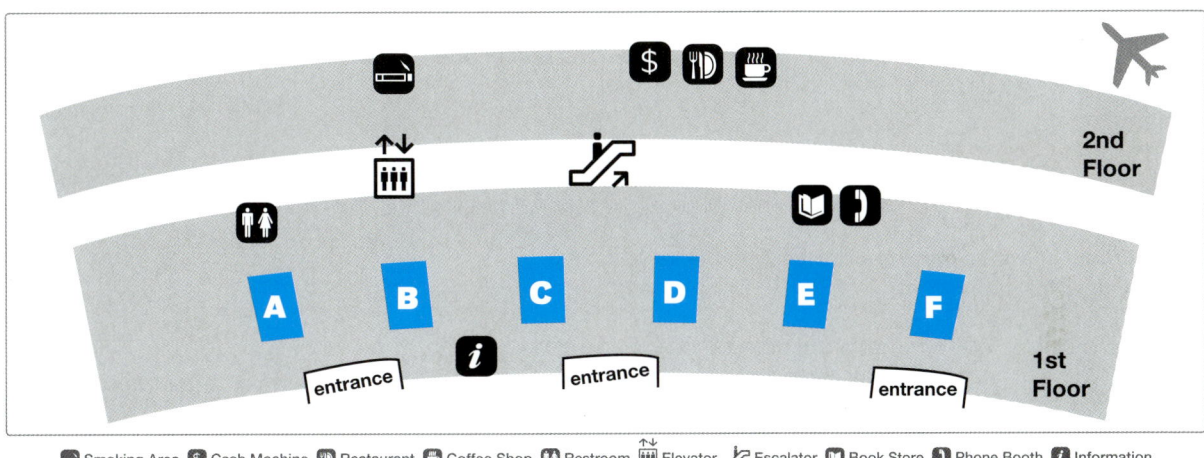

Could you tell me where the cash machine is?

Sure. There's one on the second floor. Take the escalator up to the second floor and it's next to a restaurant.

Student A:
1) You want to buy a book.
2) You want to get some money from an ATM.
3) You're hungry!

Student B:
1) You need to go to the restroom.
2) You want to buy a cup of coffee.
3) You want to make a phone call. (You don't have your cell phone.)

Conversation 2 — Out on the Street

track 12

Listen and practice with a partner.

Sarah: **Do you know how to get**[1] to the restaurant?

Sam: What does the GPS on your tablet say?

Sarah: Oh, let me put the restaurant's name in. It says to go straight one block, then **make a**[2] right.

Sam: That's not so bad.

Sarah: There's more. After making a right, we should go four more blocks, then make a left.

Sam: Is that it?

Sarah: Almost. Next we should go straight for about half a kilometer until we get to a five-way intersection. **We should go straight**[3] through the intersection. The restaurant will be **the second building on the left**[4].

Sam: That's pretty far. Should we take a taxi?

1 Do you know the way | Do you have directions | I'm not sure how to get (*not a question*)
2 take a | hang a | go
3 We're supposed to continue straight | We keep going straight | Then it's straight
4 next to the drugstore just after the corner | across the street from a movie theater | on the right, just 30 meters from the intersection

Pair Work

Look at the map with a partner and complete the sentences.

| just before | straight ahead | at the end of the block |
| just past | kitty-corner to | in the middle of the next/second block |

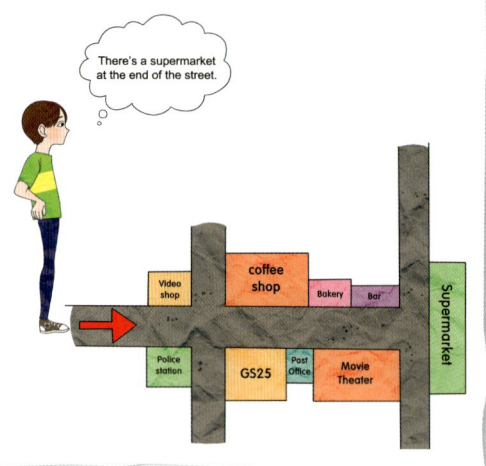

1 There's a supermarket _____.
2 There's a movie theater _____ the post office.
3 There's a coffee shop _____ the police station.
4 There's a convenience store _____ the post office.
5 There's a bakery _____.
6 There's a video shop _____.

Speaking for Everyday Life 1

Which Exit?

You have just arrived in a popular place in your city by subway. You are there to meet a friend, but you don't know where he/she is. Call him/her and ask for directions. Your partner should tell you which exit to use. (Take turns: Student B turn to page 109.)

> Your partner wants to meet in these places.
> Give him/her for directions from the subway.

Starry Coffeeshop   Milan bakery   1st bank   Alfredo's Spaghetti   movie theater

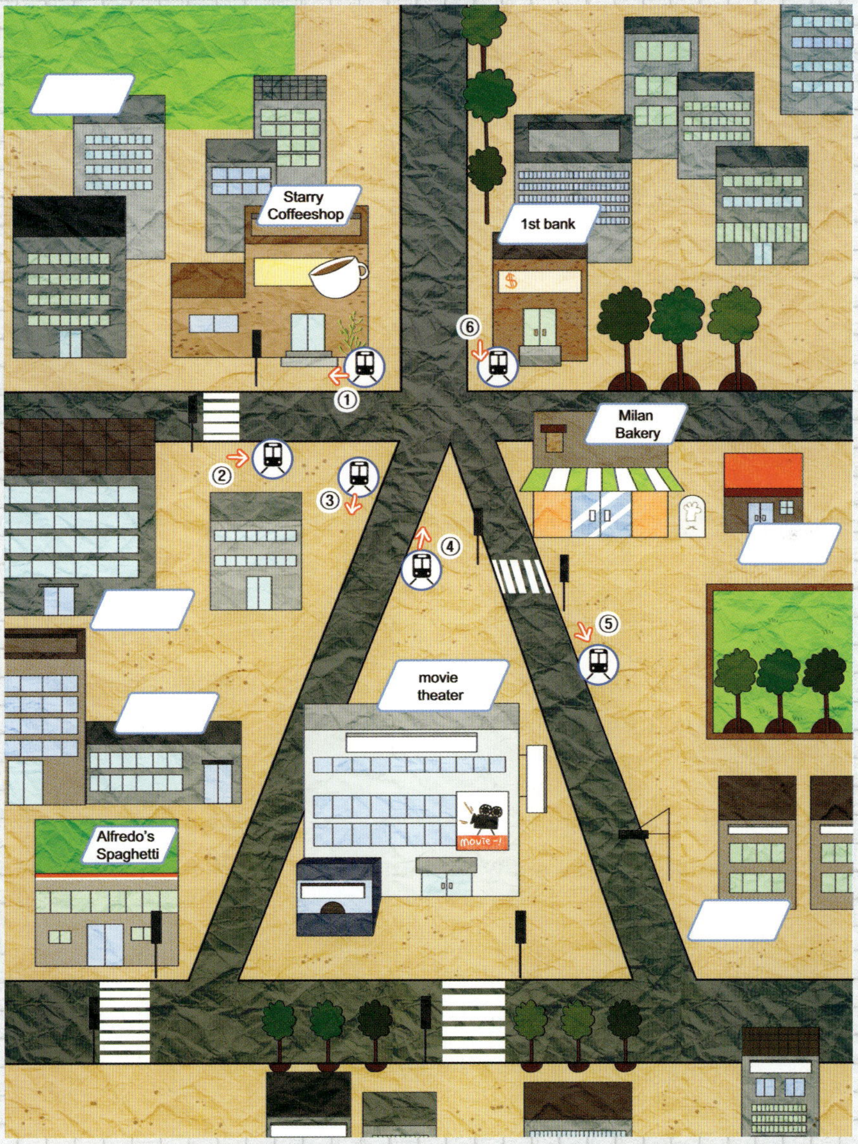

Listening Activity

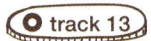

Listen to the conversation and write down the letter that matches the place.

1 taxi stand _____   2 bus stop _____   3 money changer _____

Common Mistakes!

When Korean students give directions in English, the three most common mistakes they make are outlined below:

	Konglish to English	Grammar Points
1	At the first intersection, *you* turn left. (X) → At the first intersection, turn left. (O)	When giving directions, make sure you use the imperative form.
2	Turn right at the corner. The bakery *is* on your left. (X) → Turn right at the corner. The bakery *will be* on your left. (O)	Also, use future tense to describe what people will see if they follow your directions.
3	Go to the intersection, then *across* the street. (X) → Go to the intersection, then *cross* the street. (O) → Go to the intersection, then *go across* the street. (O)	Korean students are often confused with *across* (adverb) and *cross* (verb).

Writing Activity — *How Do You Get to Your Home?*

For homework, draw a simple map to your home from the nearest subway station or bus stop. Bring your map to class and explain how to get to your home from the nearest subway station or bus stop.

- Draw an X to show where you live.
- Use a square to show the nearest subway of bus stop.
- Include several landmarks to help the person follow the correct path.
  (convenience stores, churches, large apartment buildings, etc.)

↑ North

Wrap-it-up Questions

Get into groups of four. Turn to 'Wrap-it-up Questions' in the back of this book. Students should ONLY look at their own questions.

UNIT 04 Entertainment and Leisure

In this unit, you will learn how to:
- talk about common hobbies
- invite someone to do something
- accept/decline/reschedule an invitation

Starter | Making Invitations

Ask your partner(s) if they like the activities pictured below, then make invitations.

> *Do you like swimming? How about going swimming this Saturday?*

1. hiking, this Sunday

2. skiing, this weekend

3. playing computer games, online sometime

4. shopping, after class

34 Speaking for Everyday Life 1

Vocabulary

A Fill in the blanks with the correct expressions.

> turn down   accept   get together   hobby   reschedule   hanging out

1. When you agree to do something with a friend, you _____ their invitation.
2. When you refuse to do something with a friend, you _____ their invitation.
3. When you change the time of an appointment, you _____ it.
4. If you spend time doing a certain activity for pleasure, it is your _____.
5. When you spend time alone or with your friends doing nothing special, you are _____.
6. Many students like to _____ with their friends on the weekend.

B Match the hobby on the left with the definition on the right.

1. martial arts
2. sewing
3. blogging
4. water skiing
5. hiking
6. playing Go
7. scuba diving
8. mountain climbing
9. cooking
10. yoga
11. cycling
12. photography

- ⓐ walking in the country, forests, or mountains
- ⓑ skiing on lakes or rivers in warm weather
- ⓒ swimming underwater using special equipment
- ⓓ sports like taekwondo, judo, karate, etc.
- ⓔ going up and down mountains with special equipment
- ⓕ making clothes, blankets, etc. yourself, by hand
- ⓖ writing an online journal for others to read
- ⓗ game using a board and many black and white beads
- ⓘ exercises for stretching the body and relaxing the mind
- ⓙ riding a bicycle for fun and exercise
- ⓚ making food for people to enjoy
- ⓛ taking pictures for fun or work

Conversation 1 — Talking about Hobbies

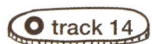

Listen and practice with a partner.

Sally: What do you do in your **free time**[1]?

Steve: I'm into sports and working out. **I really like**[2] basketball. How about you?

Sally: **I don't really like**[3] sports. I'd rather relax and watch a movie.

Steve: Really? What kind do you like?

Sally: I really like documentaries. Do you like movies?

Steve: Sure. There's a school film festival this weekend. Want to go?

Sally: Sounds great. Text me on Friday.

1 spare time | down time
2 I'm really into … | I enjoy … | I love …
3 I'm not into … | I don't like … | I really don't like … | I hate …

Grammar Points — Likes / Dislikes

Likes		Dislikes
I kind of like it. / I sort of like it.	weak	I don't really like it.
I like it.	↓	I don't like it.
I really like it.	strong	I really don't like it.
I love it!		I hate it!

A First, make four interesting *Do you like~?* questions. Second, ask a partner your questions and write down your partner's answers.

1 Q: _____ A: _____

2 Q: _____ A: _____

3 Q: _____ A: _____

4 Q: _____ A: _____

NOTE

Do you like movies?	Yes, I like movies. (OK)
Do you like to watch movies?	Yes, I like to watch movies. (OK)
Do you like watching movies?	Yes, I like watching movies. (OK)
Do you like to watching movies?	(NOT OK!)

Practice

A With a partner, make your own dialog(s) like the one on the previous page. Use some of the phrases below to help you.

- A *What do you do in your free time?*
- B *I usually...*
- A *Do you like...?*
- B *I really like... / I'm not into...*
- A *Who/What is your favorite...?*
- B *My favorite... is...*

A: _____

B: _____

A: _____

B: _____

A: _____

B: _____

B Below are some common things people don't like. Check the appropriate column for each one, then compare your answers with a partner/group.

	no problem	don't really like it	really don't like it	hate it
1 spitting				
2 knuckle cracking				
3 burping				
4 public nose-blowing				
5 leg shaking/jiggling				
6 nose picking				
7 farting				
8 loudly chewing gum				
9 smoking				
10 _____ (your choice)				

Conversation 2 — Let's Get Together

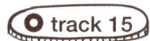 track 15

Listen and practice with a partner.

Scott: **Are you busy**[1] after class tomorrow night? I want to try that new sushi place.

Marisa: I **have plans**[2] after class. **How about**[3] this weekend?

Scott: Sounds good. I've got to work on Saturday, so how about Sunday?

Marisa: Sunday **is good**[4]. After we eat, how about going bowling?

Scott: That works. I'll call you on Sunday.

1 Are you free … | Do you have any time …
2 … am busy … | … don't have any time …
3 What about …? | Will … work? | Would … be okay?
4 … works for me | … is fine | … sounds good/great

Practice

Make dialogs like the one above using the following information.

1

Peter
Busy Friday night, wants to go hiking Saturday or Sunday

Vicky
Busy Friday night, Saturday morning, wants to take a cooking class this weekend

2

Jennifer
Busy Sunday, wants to go to a basketball game on Saturday afternoon

Dave
Busy Friday and Sunday, wants to see a movie

3

You
_____

Your Partner
_____

Activity: How about...?

Use the pictures and expressions below to make invitations. Use a DIFFERENT EXPRESSION for each invitation. Then invite your partner to do the activities. He or she will accept or decline.

1

A: How about watching a movie tonight?
B: Sounds great! | Sorry, I'm busy.

2

A: _____
B: _____

3

A: _____
B: _____

4

A: _____
B: _____

NOTE
For "How about …" or "What about …" your verb will need an 'ing'. (e.g. watching, going)

Class Activity

A Write down your class schedule and other things you have to do next week. Then write down three things you want to do next week on the DAY and TIME you want to do them.

	Monday	Tuesday	Wednesday	Thursday	Friday
morning			*quiz*		
afternoon					
evening					

B Stand up and, using your list of things you want to do, make plans with three DIFFERENT classmates. You may need to change the times to match when your classmate is free. You MUST SAY NO to at least one person – either because you don't like the activity or because you don't have time.

UNIT 04 Entertainment and Leisure

Listening Activity

A Listen and fill in the blanks. 	track 16

Kathy: Do you like to _____?
Al: Sure. I like to do yoga and _____. How _____ you?
Kathy: I love to _____ on weekends. I also _____ martial arts.
Al: I like to _____ too! Maybe we can go together sometime.

B Listen to the rest of the conversation and answer the questions. 	track 17

1. When is Kathy going skiing?
2. Does she invite Al to go with her?
3. What is Al doing?
4. Will Al go with Kathy this time? In the future?

Common Mistakes!

Change the Konglish expressions to English ones.

1. Let's see an *SF* movie. → Let's see a _____ movie.
2. Let's *play pocketball*. → Let's _____.
3. Let's *play bowling*. → Let's _____.
4. I have a *2 p.m. promise*. → I have a(n) _____.
5. Let's *Dutch pay* lunch. → Let's _____ lunch.
6. I *played* with *my* friend. → I _____ with _____ friend.
7. The movie made me *boring*. → The movie made me _____.

40 Speaking for Everyday Life 1

Writing Activity

A You have recently gone abroad to study and want to go online to make some new English-speaking friends. Write your answers to the questions below.

Favorite movie:	_____	Favorite food:	_____
Favorite TV show:	_____	Favorite actor:	_____
Favorite color:	_____	Favorite music:	_____
Least favorite food:	_____	Least favorite music:	_____

What do you like to do in your free time?
↳ _____

Why? _____

What is something you hate to do in your free time?
↳ _____

Why? _____

What new hobby would you like to try in the future?
↳ _____

Why? _____

B Now get into groups and compare your answers. Do you have similar likes/dislikes with anyone in your group?

Wrap-it-up Questions

Get into groups of four. Turn to 'Wrap-it-up Questions' in the back. Students should ONLY look at their own questions.

UNIT 05 Holidays and Family

In this unit, you will learn how to:
- talk about days of the week and months of the year
- describe Korean holidays in English
- use family-related vocabulary

Telling Dates

A
When are the special days below? Ask and answer with a partner.

1. A: When is Valentine's Day?
   B: It's on _____.

2. A: When is Thanksgiving Day?
   B: It's on _____.

3. A: When is Christmas?
   B: It's on _____.

4. A: When is Halloween?
   B: It's on _____.

B
Ask and answer with a partner.

A: *When are the important days in your life?*
B:

A: *What do you do on those days?*
B:

42 Speaking for Everyday Life 1

Vocabulary

A Fill in the blanks with the correct words.

> April Fool's Day   solar calendar   Valentine's Day   White Day
> Arbor Day   day off   lunar calendar

1 Some Korean holidays, like Chuseok, are according to a special* _____.
2 Most Western holidays are according to the _____.
3 A day you don't have to go to class or work is a _____.
4 A special day to go on a date or to give someone chocolate is _____.
5 A special day to plant trees is _____.
6 A day to play a joke on your teacher or a friend is _____.
7 A special day, common in Korea and Japan, when men give candy to women is _____.

NOTE There are several types of lunar calendars in the world.

B Dates in English are pronounced differently for different numbers. Also, there are various ways you can say dates. Fill in the blanks below and practice saying the dates.

1 1/1/2014 = January first two-thousand fourteen = the _____ of January twenty-fourteen

2 4/2/2002 = April second two-thousand two = the _____ of April twenty-oh-two

3 11/3/2050 = November _____ two thousand fifty = the third _____ November twenty-fifty

4 8/15/2021 = _____ fifteenth two thousand twenty one = the _____

C Your teacher will say the phrases below. Listen and repeat. For homework, use the CD to listen and repeat. Try to distinguish between the teens and multiples of ten.

 track 18

> 13th / the 30th of   February 13th / 2016 the 30th of February   the 18th / the 80th
>
> 10. 18. 2043 / the 80th anniversary   the 14th / the 40th   on the 14th / It's my 40th birthday.
>
> 13 / 30   14 / 40   15 / 50   16 / 60   17 / 70   18 / 80   19 / 90

Now listen to the CD for all the teens paired with multiples of ten. Practice!

Conversation 1 — White Day

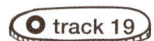 track 19

Listen and practice with a partner.

Jane: Do you have anything special planned for March 14th?

James: March 14th? What's that?

Jane: It's White Day. **When[1] guys give their girlfriends candy.**

James: You mean Valentine's Day? That was last month, Feb. 14th. I gave my girl some chocolates.

Jane: Oh, it's different in Korea. On Valentine's Day, girls give their boyfriends chocolate and on White Day, boys give their girls hard candy.

James: That sounds good for the boys! **How did that tradition get started[2]?**

Jane: Many people say candy companies made White Day to sell more candy.

James: **That's interesting![3]**

---

1. It's a day when | On this day, | The tradition is that
2. What's the origin of that day? | Why did people start doing that? | What's the history of that tradition?
3. You learn something new every day! | I didn't know that! | I've never heard that before!

Grammar Point — Time Prepositions

on + day, date	in + month, year	for + holiday, time period
I'll call you on Friday.	Christmas is in December.	What are you doing for New Year's?
Christmas is on Dec. 25th.	I was born in 1992.	We're going skiing for the weekend.

A Answer each question below.

1. When is your birthday? → _____?
2. When are you free during the week? → _____?
3. When will you graduate? → _____?
4. What are your plans for Solnal? → _____?
5. When is Chuseok this year? → _____?

Activity — When Is...?

A With a partner, complete the calendar by asking about the events listed below. (Student B turns to page 108.)

When is Hyun-ah's birthday party?

It's on Friday, the 5th.

Ask B when these events are:
- the test
- Tae-hun's birthday
- the school festival
- the Girl's Gen concert

Student A's Calendar

SUN	MON	TUE	WED	THU	FRI	SAT
	1	2	3	4	5 Hyun-ah's birthday	6
7	8	9	10 presentation	11	12	13
14	15	16	17	18	19	20 baseball game
21	22	23	24	25	26	27 Sang-kyu's wedding
28	29	30				

B In the box below, write down *OK* or *Not OK* depending on whether the question is acceptable or not. Some ideas may fit both cultures.

	Holidays	Korea	English-speaking Countries
1	Christmas is mainly a family holiday.		
2	People celebrate White Day.		
3	There is a Children's Day.		
4	Mother's Day and Father's Day are on different days.		
5	Thanksgiving (or Chuseok) is mainly a family holiday.		
6	There is a special day to honor the country's writing system.		
7	Some important holidays are scheduled according to the lunar calendar.		
8	On April Fool's Day, people usually play jokes on their friends or family, not their teachers.		
9	Many holidays are on fixed days (e.g. 4th Thursday of November) rather than dates (e.g. July 4th)		

Conversation 2 — How Big Is Your Family?

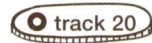

Listen and practice with a partner.

Kathrine: **What are your plans**[1] for Chuseok?

Ji-hoon: My whole family gets together at my parent's house every year for Chuseok.

Kathrine: **Do you have many brothers and sisters?**[2]

Ji-hoon: One older sister and one younger brother. I'm a middle child. My uncle's family and my grandparents on my father's side will be there also.

Kathrine: That's a lot of people.

Ji-hoon: Yes, Chuseok is an important holiday in Korea. It's like Thanksgiving for you, right? Does your family get together?

Kathrine: Yes, if we can. My **older brother and sister-in-law**[3] came over last year. Not as big as your family gathering!

1 Got any plans | What are you doing
2 How big is your family? | Do you have a large family?
3 younger sister and her fiancé | twin sister and my cousins

NOTE
Be careful not to say "How many families do you have?" It's Konglish.

Class Activity

Fill in the blanks with the names of your classmates. Use some of the new expressions below to help you.

	3 or less	4 to 5	6 or more
❶ family members			
❷ live with	grandparents	sister-in-law / brother-in-law	nephew/niece
❸ position	the oldest / the youngest	a middle child	only child

Useful Expressions

- Who do you live with?
- Are you a middle child?
- Are you the oldest?
- Are you an only child?

46 Speaking for Everyday Life 1

Activity | Family Tree

A Fill in the blanks with the correct letters.

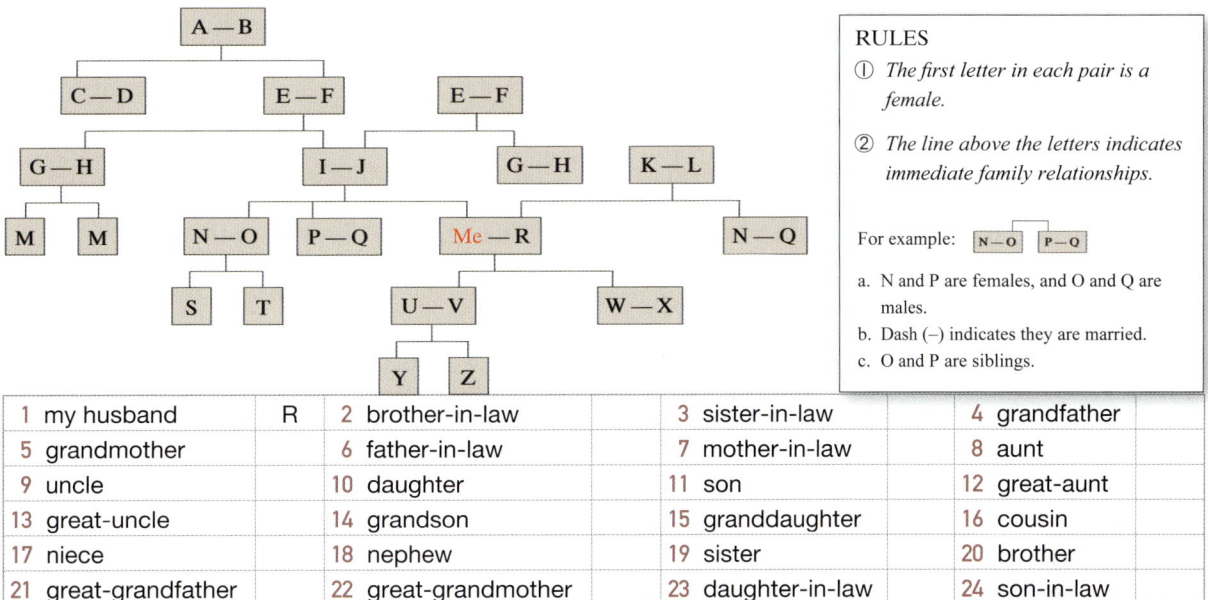

RULES
① The first letter in each pair is a female.
② The line above the letters indicates immediate family relationships.

For example: N—O P—Q

a. N and P are females, and O and Q are males.
b. Dash (–) indicates they are married.
c. O and P are siblings.

1 my husband	R	2 brother-in-law		3 sister-in-law		4 grandfather	
5 grandmother		6 father-in-law		7 mother-in-law		8 aunt	
9 uncle		10 daughter		11 son		12 great-aunt	
13 great-uncle		14 grandson		15 granddaughter		16 cousin	
17 niece		18 nephew		19 sister		20 brother	
21 great-grandfather		22 great-grandmother		23 daughter-in-law		24 son-in-law	

B In the box below write down *yes* or *no* depending on whether the idea fits that culture. Some ideas may fit both cultures.

Family Culture	Korea	English-speaking Countries
1 People of the same generation in a family often have the same first name.		
2 It's common to call an uncle or aunt by their name – like 'Uncle Ken' or 'Aunt Diane'.		
3 Traditionally, when a woman gets married, she leaves her family home and moves into her husband's.		
4 It's common to move out of the family home right after high school.		
5 The oldest son often lives with his parents even after he gets married.		
6 The whole family usually gets together at Christmas.		
7 People call their older brother or sister by their first name.		

Listening Activity

A Listen and answer the questions.   ◯ track 21

1 What year was his dad born in? His dad was born in _____.
2 What is his dad's birthday? His dad's birthday is _____.
3 What year was his grandpa born in? His grandfather was born in _____.
4 What month was his grandpa born in? His grandfather was born in _____.
5 What date was his grandpa born on? His grandfather was born on _____.

B Listen to the rest of the conversation and fill in the blanks.   ◯ track 22

Mom: Are there any other _____ you want to know?
Son: Yes, can you tell me the birthdays for Grandma and _____?
Mom: Well, Grandma was born on _____, 1952.
Son: Okay, got it. And Granny?
Mom: Let's see. She was born on _____, 1948.
Son: Okay, thanks Mom. Now I have everyone's birthday.
Mom: Good—now you won't _____ to send birthday cards!

NOTE
Many Americans distinguish between their two sets of grandparents by calling them different names such as Grandma, Granny, Grammy, Nana, Grams, or Grandpa, Grampy, Pappy, Papa. Also, when using these terms in the same way as someone's name, capitalize them just as you would a person's name.

Common Mistakes!

Change the Konglish expressions to English ones.

1 I'll visit my *big* uncle's house for Chuseok. → I'll visit my _____ uncle's house for Chuseok.
2 *I have five families.* → _____.
3 I'd like to introduce *our* wife. → I'd like to introduce _____ wife.
4 What *is your plan* for Christmas? → What _____ your _____ for Christmas?
5 *Older brother*, where are you going? → _____*, where are you going?
6 She is my *elder** sister. → She is my _____ sister.

NOTE
* 'Elder' is not wrong, it's just not common.

48 Speaking for Everyday Life 1

Writing Activity — *Your Own Family Tree*

Make your own family tree. Start with your grandparents (both sides). Do you know everyone's name? If you know the name, include it.

Father's Side

grandfather ——— grandmother

| Leroy | | |

Mother's Side

grandfather ——— grandmother

Wrap-it-up Questions

Get into groups of four. Turn to 'Wrap-it-up Questions' in the back of this book. Students should ONLY look at their own questions.

UNIT 06 Dating

In this unit, you will learn how to:
- describe appearance
- describe personality
- tell stories about past events

Starter   Describing People

A With a partner, describe the people below. Use the example sentences to help you.

He's kind of thick and short.   She's tall and really thin.   _____

_____   _____   _____

B Tell a partner about your best friend or your family members.

A What's your sister like?

B She's normal height but really fit. She's funny sometimes but usually kind of quiet.

50 Speaking for Everyday Life 1

Vocabulary

Use the adjectives below to describe appearance and personality.

	Appearance	**Personality**
	Body Type	**Personality**
He's She's	tall	outgoing
She's kind of * He's sort of * He's really * She's very *	*average-height short thin skinny heavy thick chubby well-built fit muscular	charming adventurous kind shy quiet sweet nice gentle talkative hot-tempered stuck-up moody stubborn wild funny boring grumpy
	Age	
	young old *in his/her 20s (30s, teens, etc.)	
	Facial Features	
	cute handsome beautiful pretty plain average-looking ugly	

NOTE

Don't match the asterisks in this column with the adjectives in the next column.

Conversation 1 — Set Me Up!

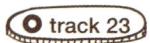

Listen and practice with a partner.

Mee-jeong: I'd really like to **meet someone**[1].

Tae-kyun: How about my buddy Mark? He's kind of short, but fit and super smart.

Mee-jeong: I think we met before. He's kind of cute, with short hair and glasses?

Tae-kyun: Right. I can **set you up**[2] next weekend.

Mee-jeong: I don't know. **What's his personality like**[3]?

Tae-kyun: He's really funny around friends, but shy around new people.

1 find someone | have/get/find a boyfriend/girlfriend*
2 introduce you | fix you up | set it up
3 What's he like | What kind of person/guy is he

NOTE
"make a boyfriend/girlfriend" is Konglish and sounds strange in English.

Practice — What's Your Type?

A Write down descriptive details of your ideal partner and nightmare partner in the chart below. Use the vocabulary section to help you. Then compare with a partner.

	Body Type	Height	Facial Features	Personality
(ideal)				
(nightmare)				

B With a partner, write the questions for the answers below. Then ask each other questions about your ideal and nightmare types. When you're finished, try asking your teacher.

1 He/She is fit and tall.   _What does he/she look like_ ?

2 He/She is 178cm tall.   _____ ?

3 He/She is very cute.   _____ ?

4 He/She is funny and smart.   _____ ?

Activity | Matchmaker

A   In groups, read the 'personal ads' below and decide who makes the best match(es).

> *I think Sam is a good match for Josie.*

Sam: I am a fun-loving, adventurous guy who would like to meet an outgoing, attractive woman. She must be someone who likes adventurous sports like river rafting or hot air ballooning. But I hope she also likes getting dressed up and trying out exciting, new restaurants! I definitely would like to settle down one day with the right woman and have a beautiful family.

Mark: Hello! I consider myself attractive, self-confident, and very passionate, both in business and in relationships. I am a successful, self-made businessman, but I am still looking for Ms. Right. I would like to meet a successful, independent woman who wants to settle down and have a family. I hope she will be honest, hardworking, and has a good job and education.

Josie: I love animals and have a dog that I love to go on hikes or camping in the mountains with. I love the outdoors, but sometimes I like to stay inside to watch a movie, listen to music, or just relax. But I also like to go out with my friends and have a lot of laughs. I'm only interested in meeting serious, mature men.

Linda: I'm looking for a dynamic, fit, professional man. He should know how to separate his business life from his personal life. I am a professional woman (lawyer) who works hard and needs to have more fun. I speak Spanish, play pool, cook, dance, and travel when I can. Although I argue for a living, I leave that at the office – at home I am a real sweetie.

B   In two or three sentences write a short personal ad about yourself or someone you know.

_____

_____

C   Next, get with a partner and decide who (someone in class, a movie star or TV character, someone from a book, etc.) would be a good match for your personal ad.

Conversation 2 — How Did Your Date Go?

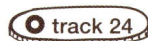

Listen and practice with a partner.

Sam: Tell me about your date last night.

Sherri: It was good at first. We were talking and having coffee at that new coffee shop near school when ①**his ex-girlfriend walked in**!

Sam: Really? What happened next?

Sherri: ②**He tried to ignore her, but she came over to our table**!

Sam: What happened then?

Sherri: ③**She dumped coffee on his head**! I couldn't believe it!

Situation 1	Situation 2
① there was a car accident just outside the coffee shop ② The guy I was with, Steve, ran out to help ③ He pulled an old lady from the car just before it caught on fire	*Students' choice*

Grammar Points — Simple Past vs. Past Progressive

A When talking about past events, it's common to mix simple past tense with past progressive. Past progressive is commonly used for actions that are happening when another, more sudden action, occurs.

Past Progressive		Simple Past
I was sitting in class		the teacher **called** my name.
He was watching TV	*when*	you **called** him.
We were having dinner		the robber **broke** into the house.
She was listening to music		the phone **rang**.

NOTE: It's also common to use past progressive with sentences using 'while' or 'as'.
Ex. As I was taking a shower, someone rang the doorbell. Someone knocked on my door while I was sleeping.

B Next, write two phrases in past progressive, similar to the examples here.

_____

_____

C Now, get with a partner and write Ssimple past phrases to finish the new sentences.

Activity: How My Parents First Met

Fill in the blanks with the verbs indicated. For the italic verbs, use past progressive. Use simple past for the other verbs.

My parents 1 _____ (meet) at a public car wash. While my mother 2 _____ (*wash*) her car, my father 3 _____ (*wait*) to wash his car. They 4 _____ (do) not know each other. My mother 5 _____ (*clean*) her car too slowly. My father 6 _____ (get) angry and 7 _____ (say), "Hurry up!" My mother, who has a hot temper, 8 _____ (say), "If you don't like it, you wash it!" Then she 9 _____ (throw) her wet towel at my father and 10 _____ (walk) away. My father 11 _____ (be) surprised, but he 12 _____ (do not have) time to argue. He quickly 13 _____ (wash) my mother's car. Then he 14 _____ (move) her car, 15 _____ (wash) his own car and 16 _____ (leave). A few days later, while my father 17 _____ (*work*), he 18 _____ (think) about what happened and 19 _____ (laugh). He 20 _____ (decide) he 21 _____ (want) to meet my mother again. At that time, they 22 _____ (live) in a small town. My father 23 _____ (ask) his friends and family about the woman and her car. Someone 24 _____ (know) her name. My father 25 _____ (call) my mother and 26 _____ (ask) her for a date.

Pair Work: What Were You Doing When…?

Look at the pictures and sentence starters and make up what happened for each picture.

1

We were studying when

_____.

2

They were paying when

_____.

3

I was driving when

_____.

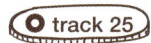

Listen to the two conversations and fill in the chart.

	Appearance	Personality
Sam		
Susan		

Common Mistakes!

In the box below, write down *yes* or *no* depending on whether the idea fits that culture. Some ideas may fit both cultures. There may be *NO RIGHT* answer, the chart is mainly for discussion purposes.

	Dating	Korea	English-speaking Countries
1	Blind dates, especially among college students, are very common.		
2	It's rare for a woman to ask out a man.		
3	Men nearly always pay for dates.		
4	Walking in the rain is romantic.		
5	Meeting your boy/girlfriend's parents usually means you are getting married soon.		
6	A romantic weekend trip is common – even for unmarried college couples.		
7	It's common to use online dating sites.		
8	Many people use professional matchmakers to find a husband/wife.		
9	Weddings, including the reception, last several hours.		
10	You can usually know if someone is married by looking at the ring finger of their left hand.		

Writing Activity — A Romantic First Meeting

A Write a short story like the one on page 55 about how your parents, or you and your boy/girlfriend, first met. Use simple past, past progressive, and short sentences.

<Useful Vocabulary>

Present – Past
- meet – met (in a coffee shop, at school, …)
- introduce – introduced (introduced A to B)
- like – liked (her when they first met…)
- drink – drank (tea, beer, soju, …)
- wear – wore (a new shirt, favorite dress, …)
- work – worked (in the same office, …)

Present – Past
- see – saw (a movie, a pretty face, a nice smile, …)
- have – had (dinner, a cup of coffee, …)
- go – went (to a party, to a restaurant, …)
- take – took (a bus, the subway, a picture, …)
- listen – listened (to music, to her/his story, …)
- live – lived (in the same town, near each other, …)

Your Parents or You & Your Boy/Girlfriend

_____
_____
_____
_____
_____
_____

B Get into groups and share your story with the other members of your group. Who has the most interesting story?

Wrap-it-up Questions

Get into groups of four. Turn to 'Wrap-it-up Questions' in the back. Students should ONLY look at their own questions.

UNIT 07
Phones and Text Messages

In this unit, you will learn how to:
- leave and take phone messages
- send text messages in English
- make polite requests

Starter

Cell Phones and the Internet

With a partner, ask and answer the questions.

1) How significant is your internet presence?
   For example, do you have your own homepage? Do you regularly use social media like Facebook?

2) How much time do you use communicating with others on the Internet?

1) Rank and discuss all the functions you use on your cell phone:
   (*write 1 for most important, 2 for next most important, etc.*)

   ____ call someone   ____ send pictures to someone

   ____ take photos   ____ get directions

   ____ surf the Internet   ____ check your email

   ____ text someone   ____ (*other*): _____

2) Do your friends get angry if you use your cell phone too much when meeting with them?

3) Do you think you have good manners when using your cell phone?
   For example, do you speak too loudly in restaurants or on the subway? Do you walk and text at the same time? Do you drive while using your cell phone?

Vocabulary

A Write the words in the box below in the blanks to match them to the correct definitions.

> missed   swipe   caller ID   mobile   caps   vibrate

1. You should not write text or Internet messages in all _____.
2. In order not to disturb others, you can set your phone to _____ mode.
3. This is how you know who is calling you. _____
4. When you drag your finger across the screen of your cell phone. _____
5. When you did not notice that someone called you, your phone will indicate that you have a _____ call.
6. Another name for your cell phone is: _____ phone.

B Look at the smartphone and find some buttons or functions with your partner.

on/off button
volume control
battery charge
signal bars
Internet search field
call button
record icon
apps

C Common reasons why someone can't take a call

I'm sorry, Ms. Kim is in a meeting.
        at lunch
        not at her desk
        on a break
        on another line

I'm sorry, Ms. Kim has not come in yet.
        gone home
        left for the day

Conversation 1 — May I Take a Message?

 track 26

Listen and practice with a partner.

Rebeca: This is Best Purchase, Rebeca Tanning here.

Seok-tae: Yes, could **you connect me**[1] to Mike in your Mobile department please?

Rebeca: I'm sorry, **Mike is off today**[2]. May I take a message?

Seok-tae: Yes, could you have him call me back tomorrow? My name is Seok-tae.

Rebeca: I'm sorry, could you spell that please?

Seok-tae: Sure, it's S-E-O-K dash T-A-E.

Rebeca: Okay, and does he have your number?

Seok-tae: He should, but just in case, it's 010-867-5309.

Rebeca: Okay, that's Seok-tae at 010-867-5309. I'll **be sure to give him your message**[3].

1 you put me through to | I speak
2 Mike is away from his desk at the moment | it's his day off today
3 let him know you called | relay your message to him

Grammar Point — Text Messaging

A Just as in Korean, English has shorter ways to write things in text messages. Match the proper English expression with the shorter expressions used in texting.

1 ;-) CU L8R   ·   · ⓐ In my humble opinion, …
2 OMG, TMI   ·   · ⓑ (wink) See you later.
3 IMHO   ·   · ⓒ Oh my god, that's too much information.
4 M$ULkeCrZ..:)   ·   · ⓓ Out of the office, call me at 2.
5 brb   ·   · ⓔ I'll be right back.
6 OOTO..CM@2   ·   · ⓕ Miss you like crazy. (smile)
7 WAYD   ·   · ⓖ What are you doing?

B Now try sending a text message, IN ENGLISH, to another student in class. Your teacher may ask you what you sent, or if you got an answer.

Short Phone Conversations

With a partner, read the dialogs and fill in the blanks. Then answer the questions. (Student B turns to page 111.)

Reserving a Table at a Restaurant

You call to reserve a table at a popular restaurant. You want to eat between 7 and 8 p.m. and there will be five people in your group. Make sure the restaurant has a table at that time and confirm the information.

Head Waiter:	_____?
You:	Yes, I would like to reserve a table at 7 p.m.
Head Waiter:	_____.
You:	That's fine. Please reserve one under the name Dunaway.
Head Waiter:	_____?
You:	Five.
Head Waiter:	_____.
You:	That's right. Thank you very much. We'll see you at 8.

- What is the name of the restaurant?
- When is a table available?
- Why are there no tables available at 7 p.m.?

Texting and Calling a Friend

You are trying to call your friend, but his/her phone seems to be off. You text him/her instead. You want to meet him/her for dinner next week.

You:	(text)	Hey, WAYD? Ur phone goes to recording.
Your Friend:	(text)	_____.
Your Friend:	(answering phone)	_____.
You:		Hi, I didn't know you were in Japan.
Your Friend:		_____.
You:		Want to go to dinner on Friday night? I was thinking barbeque.
Your Friend:		_____.

- Why does the phone go to a recording when someone calls?
- Where is the friend now?
- When will the friend return?

Conversation 2 — Could You Help Me?

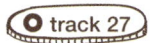 track 27

Listen and practice with a partner.

Bert: Hey Sara, **could you help me out**[1]?

Sara: Sure, **what's up**[2]?

Bert: I'm trying to **take a picture with my phone**[3], but **I can't turn on the flash**[4]. Do you know how to do that?

Sara: Yeah, I think so. Let me see your phone. Okay, push this button here. Then touch the screen and hold for a few seconds. Now **you're all set**[5].

Bert: Oh, that was easy! Thanks!

1 could you do me a favor | can you help me with something
2 what can I do for you | how can I help
3 turn off roaming service on my phone | install an app on my phone
4 it doesn't seem to be letting me do that | it isn't downloading
5 it's off | you can use it

Pair Work — Polite Requests

A Look at the map with a partner and complete the sentences.

Polite Requests	Possible Answers
Could you have her call me back?	Sure.
Would you let her know I called?	No problem.
Would you please close the window?	Yes, I can do that.
Would you mind if I borrowed your car?	Well, if you promise to be careful.

NOTE
Usually, more difficult requests are made with more polite and complicated expressions.

B Use the pictures below to ask for favors from your partner. Be creative. Take turns asking and answering.

Activity | I'm Hot!

Imagine you and your partner are in the situations below. Use 'could you' polite requests to try to take care of the problems.

> Could you turn on the air-conditioning?
>
> Sure, no problem.

1. You are a passenger in your friend's car. You are hot. The air-conditioning is off.
2. You are visiting your colleague's house. You need to use the bathroom.
3. You are calling an important client. Her secretary says that she is in a meeting.
4. You are sitting in class. It's winter, and you are cold. The window next to the teacher is open.
5. You want to buy a drink from a vending machine, but you don't have any small bills. All you have is one 10,000 won bill. The machine only takes 1,000 won bills or coins. You see a friend.

Pair Work | Polite Refusals

A Match the request with the appropriate polite refusal.

1. Could you show me how to use this?
2. Would you lend me some money?
3. Could I use your battery charger?
4. Would you mind giving me a ride?

ⓐ I would, but my car is in the shop.
ⓑ I'm sorry, but I'm using it now.
ⓒ I'm sorry, but I'm late for class.
ⓓ I'm sorry, but I'm broke.

B Write down requests that match the polite refusals below.

1. A: _____?

   B: I'm sorry, I don't have enough change to break a 1,000 won bill.

2. A: _____?

   B: I'm sorry, but the battery in my laptop is almost dead.

3. A: _____?

   B: I'm sorry, but one, I'm busy this weekend, and two, the last time I helped someone move, I hurt my back.

A **Listen and fill in the message note below.**

Message

To : ① _____

Mr. / Ms.: ② _____

　　✓　called　　　　　　　　　　_____ please call back

　　___ stopped by　　　　　　　 _____ will call back

Message: ③ _____

_____

_____

B **Listen one more time and answer the questions.**

1 Who is the message for?　　　　　　　_____

2 Who is the message from?　　　　　　_____

3 Who took the message?　　　　　　　_____

4 Why can't the person come to the phone?　_____

5 Will the caller call again?　　　　　　_____

Common Mistakes!

Change the Konglish expressions to English ones.

1 I lost my *handphone*.　　　　　　　　→　I lost my _____.

2 You should not *texting* while driving.　→　You should not _____ while driving.

3 Could you give me a 7 a.m. *morning call*?　→　Could you give me a 7 a.m. _____?

4 I need to take my phone to the *A/S center*.　→　I need to take my phone to the _____.

5 May I take *your* message?　　　　　　→　May I take _____ message?

Writing Activity

We learned some basic 'text message style' English on page 92. Here we will practice it some more. Write down four text messages below. Then exchange books with a partner. Can you understand what your partner wrote? If you can, write a response.

Messages

1. _____
2. _____
3. _____
4. _____

Responses

1. _____
2. _____
3. _____
4. _____

Wrap-it-up Questions

Get into groups of four. Turn to 'Wrap-it-up Questions' in the back. Students should ONLY look at their own questions.

UNIT 08 Jobs

In this unit, you will learn how to:
- use 'can'
- respond to common interview questions
- write basic résumé writing

Starter — Job Experience

A Did you ever have a part-time job? What did you do?

> A I am/was <u>a server at a restaurant downtown</u>.

server/waiter/waitress   barista   tutor   store clerk

B What kind of job do you want in the future? Is it related to your major?

> A I want to be a(n) _____.   B It's (not) related to my major.

You: _____

Your Partner: _____

C Where do you want to work – at a big company? For the government? Overseas? Freelance? Start your own company? Family business?

> A I want to work for the government because…
>
> B I want to start my own company because…

You: _____

Your Partner: _____

66 Speaking for Everyday Life 1

Vocabulary

A Fill in the blanks with the correct words.

> résumé   reference   PhD/doctorate   summer job   full-time job
> Bachelor's Degree (BA or BS)   Master's Degree (MA, MS, or MBA)

1 A _____ details your education, work experience, and other important information.

2 The opposite of a part-time job is a _____.

3 A job you only have during summer vacation can be called a _____.

4 After you graduate from four years of college, you will get a diploma and a _____.

5 After graduation from college, if you study more (usually for two years) you will get a _____.

6 The highest degree is a _____.

7 A person or a kind of letter that tells people how great you are so you can get a job or into a college or graduate school is a _____.

B Draw a line from the job on the left to the description on the right.

1 chef   ⓐ tries to get people to buy things
2 civil servant   ⓑ takes care of passengers on a plane
3 salesperson   ⓒ designs machines and other things
4 engineer   ⓓ fixes machines
5 mechanic   ⓔ works as a singer, actor/actress, etc.
6 lawyer   ⓕ is a very good cook
7 manager   ⓖ works for the government
8 professor   ⓗ does research, tries to discover new things
9 entertainer   ⓘ helps clients in court or with legal problems
10 flight attendant   ⓙ helps run a department, business, or store
11 scientist   ⓚ teaches at a university
12 diplomat   ⓛ saves people from burning buildings
13 firefighter   ⓜ fights crime, also called a police officer
14 cop   ⓝ represents his/her government and country

Conversation 1 — After Graduation

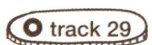

Listen and practice with a partner.

Roland: **What do you want to do**[1] when you're finished with school?

Denise: A lot of people in my family are in business, but I really want to be a flight attendant. How about you?

Roland: I'm not sure. I know I don't like my major, so probably **something besides**[2] engineering.

Denise: Any ideas?

Roland: Yeah, I think I'd like to **become**[3] a cop.

Denise: Really? Good luck. It's important to find a job you enjoy.

1 What do you want to be | Where do you want to work
2 something other than | something instead of
3 be | find work as | try becoming

Practice — Likes / Dislikes

A Make dialogs for people with the following backgrounds. Be sure the dialog changes depending on whether the job matches the major!

Kyeong-hui	Amy
Major: art	Major: business administration
Career goal: graphic designer	Career goal: writer

Cheol-soo	Dave
Major: physical education	Major: English
Career goal: singer	Career goal: English teacher

B Make your own dialog with a partner.

You	Your Partner
Major:	Major:
Career goal:	Career goal:

68 Speaking for Everyday Life 1

Activity | Job Advertisements

With a partner, take turns matching the soon-to-graduate students with their first job. (Turn to page 110 for the students' information.)

Classified Ads | Job Advertisements

Nursery School Teacher	Management Trainee	Assistant Interior Designer
Well-known nursery school seeks entry-level teacher. Must have experience with younger students, teaching degree and an outgoing personality. Salary is $32,000 a year. Call or e-mail for details.	Fast – growing restaurant franchise seeks hard-working college graduates. Must have customer service experience, prefer people with restaurant experience. Salary starts at $37,000 a year. Call or e-mail for details.	New interior design company seeks entry-level designer. Must have a design degree, experience in interior design, and an ability to work with customers. Salary depends on experience. Call or e-mail for details.

Asking about the candidate

A: What's his/her degree in?
B: His/Her degree is (will be) in art and design.
A: Tell me about her/his work experience.
B: He/She worked for 7 months at Kim's Kimbap. He/She has experience taking customer orders.

Asking about the job

A: What kind of job is it?
B: It's an opening for a nursery school teacher.
A: What kind of experience/background is required?
B: They are looking for someone with interior design experience.
A: What's the starting salary?
B: The starting salary is 30,000 dollars a year.

...is a good/bad match for the ... job opening.

1

Tom Jones

2

Bak Sun-hye

3

Choi Jin-hyuk

Conversation 2 | Job Interview

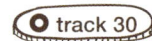

Listen and practice with a partner.

Eugene: Are you ready to practice for your interview?

Ian: Sure, what's the first question?

Eugene: Why do you want to work for our **company**[1]?

Ian: That's easy. I want to work here because I've always wanted to **work in import-export**[2] and it's a great match for my education and experience.

Eugene: Good. Next … **do you work well on a team**[3]?

Ian: In the interview I say **yes, and then provide examples from my résumé**[4].

Eugene: Great! It sounds like you understand what to do.

1 school | organization | department
2 teach English to middle school students | make the world better by working for an NGO | design and build fantastic websites
3 can you tell me one of your weaknesses | do you speak any foreign languages | do you work well with others
4 an old problem and how I overcame it | yes and give at least one language | yes and explain how and why

Grammar Points | Can You …?

Questions	Answers	
	Affirmative	_Negative_
Can you speak English? Chinese?	Yes, I can.	No, I can't.
Can you work well with other people?		
Can you use spreadsheets?		
How well can you speak English?	Well. / Very well.	A little. / Not bad.

Write down three 'can' questions below. Then practice with a partner or your teacher. Be sure to use 'How well can you ~?' as your follow-up question. Your questions can be about job interviews, or anything else you'd like to ask.

1 _____?

2 _____?

3 _____?

 **'Can you' Bingo!**

Time to practice 'can' with some more people! Stand up and ask/answer the questions below. The first one to get four names in a row is the winner. Every name must be different!

Can you cook spaghetti?	Can you send a text message in English?	Can you drive a car?	Can you swim?
Can you explain what your name traditionally means?	Can you tell a joke in English?	Can you iron a shirt?	Can you drink more than one bottle of soju?
Can you ride a bicycle?	Can you speak any Korean dialects (saturi)?	Can you make ramen?	Can you sing?
Can you speak a language besides Korean and English?	Can you rollerblade?	Can you tell me a joke?	Can you play pool?

NOTE
For example, "Yong" means "dragon" and "Miller" means someone who grinds wheat.

 **Mini Job Interview**

Now let's try a basic job interview using 'can' and some of the other expressions we've learned in this unit. One partner will be the interviewer, the other the candidate. Then switch. Be sure your questions actually match the kind of job your partner wants!

Interviewer
Tell me about your work history.
Can you speak any foreign languages? Which ones?
Can you tell me one of your weaknesses?
Can you work well with others?
_____ (make your own question)

Candidate
I can ... So I can help your ...
I can speak ...
My weakness was ... But I overcame it by ...
I can work well ... because ...

UNIT 08 Jobs 71

Listening Activity

 track 31

A Listen and answer the questions.

1. The conversation is during:

    ⓐ a date   ⓑ a job interview   ⓒ two friends drinking

2. The man has a lot of experience with full-time jobs.

    ⓐ TRUE   ⓑ FALSE

3. When did the man work more?

    ⓐ during the school year   ⓑ after graduation   ⓒ during vacations

B Listen to the rest of the conversation and fill in the blanks.

track 32

> Interviewer: I'd like to see more _____ for this position.
>
> Tae-ho: Ma'am, I have great grades, _____ letters from a professor and a former boss, and I learn fast. I'll quickly become a strong part of your _____.
>
> Interviewer: OK, good positive answer. I'll check your _____. Next question … why do you want to work for us?
>
> Tae-ho: This _____ is exactly what I've been looking for. It _____ my major, my part-time work, and I'm really interested in the field.

Common mistakes!

Change the Konglish expressions to English ones.

1. I have a good *arbeit*. → I have a good _____.
2. I want to be a good *salaryman*. → I want to be a good _____.
3. I learned a lot from my *seniors*. → I learned a lot from my _____.
4. I have a *wide* mind. → I have an _____ mind.
5. I *went to abroad* to study English. → I _____ to study English.
6. I'm *a staff* at OCC Korea. → I'm on the _____ at OCC Korea.*
7. We need *white*, *bond*, and a new *hotchkiss*. → We need _____, _____, and a new _____.

NOTE
'I work for OCC Korea.' is even better.

Writing Activity — My Resume

Look at the basic resume below carefully, then write a basic résumé about yourself.

1 Kevin Christman 010-123-4567 Kevin@SomeEmailAddress.com

2 Objective A web-design position with a well-known, international IT company

3 Education University of the Pacific   expected* February 2015
– B.S. in Computer Science

4 Experience Web Designer, University of the Pacific   Sept. 2012 – present
– help design and update school website

Clerk, Starbucks Coffee Shop   Jan. 2012 – May 2012
– served coffee to customers
– won award for customer service

NOTE: If you have not graduated, then put 'expected' in front of your future graduation date.

1 Name and Contact Information
Contact information usually means your phone number (home or cell) and your e-mail address. Sometimes people also write their address.

2 Objective
What kind of job/position do you want? What kind of company/organization do you want to work for? Write down that information here.

3 Education
It is normal for younger people to put the education part before the experience part in their resume. People with more work experience usually put experience before education. Either way, write your school name next to education. Below that, write your degree and major. On the far right, put your graduation date.

4 Work Experience
'Experience' is on the left. Then your title and the company name. Last, on the right, are the dates you worked at that place. Below the title and company, write what you did. For a past job, use the past tense. For a current job, use the present tense.

Wrap-it-up Questions

Get into groups of four. Turn to 'Wrap-it-up Questions' in the back. Students should ONLY look at their own questions.

UNIT 09 Food

In this unit, you will learn how to:
- describe food
- use countable/uncountable nouns
- use comparatives

Starter — Talking about Food

A Match the national flags with the names of each country's traditional foods. Then describe these foods to a partner. Try to use different adjectives.

sushi   hamburger   pizza   burrito

1 _____   2 _____   3 _____   4 _____

B Ask and answer the question with your partner.

A: *What do you normally eat for breakfast/lunch/dinner?*

B: *I usually eat <u>kimbap</u> for <u>breakfast</u>.*

Vocabulary

A Look at the common taste expressions.

COMPLAINTS		PRAISE	
It's too	greasy.	It's	good.
It looks	slimy disgusting gross salty sour sweet bitter spicy bland fattening	It looks	wonderful delicious scrumptious mouthwatering healthy good for you

B Match the pictures with the foods/ingredients and describe them with the adjectives above.

seaweed   egg   peppers   garlic   bean sprouts   tofu

UNIT 09 Food

Conversation 1 — How Much Should I Get?

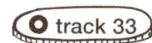 track 33

Listen and practice with a partner.

Brian: Hey, I'm coming home. Should I get anything at the store?

Sooky: Yes, we need **some milk**[1]. Could you pick up a **carton**[2]?

Brian: Sure. Do we have anything for dessert?

Sooky: Yes, we have a little fruitcake left.

Brian: Oh, yuck. You know I think that fruitcake is **disgusting**[3].

Sooky: You're weird. Anyway, that's all we have.

Brian: Okay, then I'll get some ice cream.

Sooky: Don't get too much. You're getting fat. Oh, and get **some**[4] apples.

Brian: Very funny. How many apples do we need?

Sooky: Six should be fine.

1 butter | ketchup | tofu
2 container | bottle | package
3 gross | too salty | too bland
4 a few | several | a bunch of

Grammar Points — Countable Nouns vs. Uncountable Nouns

Expressions for describing quantity vary depending on whether the noun is countable or uncountable.

COUNTABLE NOUNS	UNCOUNTABLE NOUNS
How many _____ is/are there?	How much _____ is there?
There are *some* oranges.	There is *some* cheese.
There are *a few* apples.	There is *a little* sugar.
There are *a lot of/lots of* potatoes.	There is *a lot of/lots of* coffee.
There are *several* bottles.	There is *a lot of/lots of* milk.
There are *plenty of* cookies.	There is *plenty of* chocolate.
There are *tons of* mangoes.	There is *a ton of* ice cream.
There aren't *any* tomatoes.	There isn't *any* flour.
There aren't *many* bananas.	There isn't *much** milk left.

NOTE

It's not common to use 'much' in positive statements for uncountable nouns.
Use 'a lot of' instead: I have much money. (X) → I have a lot of money.(O)
Use 'much' for negative statements: I don't have much money. (O)

Activity: In the Kitchen

Work in groups of three. Each of you is making a different meal for lunch. Ask your partners for the things you need. Just ask for one thing at a time.

A: I'm making an omelet. Does anyone have **some** eggs?
B: Not me. I don't have **any** eggs.
C: I've got **a dozen** eggs. How **many** do you need?
A: Just **two**.
C: Here you go.
A: Thanks. (Student A crosses out 'two eggs'.)
B: I'm making cheeseburgers, so I need **a lot of** ground beef. Does anyone have **any** ground beef?

Student A  You are making an omelet.

Student B   You are making cheeseburgers.

Student C You are making bibimbap.

You have:
a bunch of carrots
a head of lettuce
many tomatoes
several bottles of catsup
a ton of sliced cheese
a lot of bean sprouts
many hamburger buns

You need:
_____ eggs
_____ cheese
_____ cooking oil
_____ salt
_____ potato
_____ onion
_____ sausages

You have:
a big bag of shredded cheese
a large bottle of cooking oil
lots of cooking oil
a lot of pork
some spinach
a couple onions
a big bag of rice

You need:
_____ ground beef
_____ cheese
_____ ketchup
_____ tomatoes
_____ lettuce
_____ bacon
_____ buns

You have:
a dozen eggs
many sausages
a package of bacon
a big bag of potatoes
several tomatoes
a lot of salt
a ton of ground beef

You need:
_____ of rice
_____ pork
_____ carrots
_____ bean sprouts
_____ egg
_____ seaweed
_____ spinach

Conversation 2 | What's for Dinner?

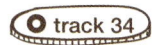
track 34

Listen and practice with a partner.

Bert: Hey Mary, how about ordering out for dinner?

Mary: Sure, we can get ① **fried chicken or pizza**.

Bert: Well, ② **fried chicken is a lot greasier than pizza**. I'm trying to lose weight.

Mary: ③ **So should I order pizza? It is tastier than fried chicken.**

Bert: Why don't we order bibimbop? It's healthier than both **chicken** and **pizza**.

Mary: That's a good idea. Do you know the number for a good Korean restaurant?

Situation 1
① hamburgers or dong-gass
② hamburgers are a lot more fattening that dong-gass
③ So should I order dong-gass? Even though it is blander than hamburgers.

Situation 2
Students' choice

Practice | Comparatives

When comparing things, such as food, there are two basic patterns to follow. A general rule is that if the adjective has less than three syllables, you add '–er' to the end. If the adjective has three or more syllables, you use the word 'more' or 'less' in front of the adjective.

less than 3 syllables: '-er'	3 syllables or more: 'more' or 'less'	special
sweet → sweeter	popular → more popular	good → better
small → smaller	delicious → more delicious	bad → worse
close → closer	comfortable → more comfortable	fun → more/less fun
old → older	expensive → less expensive	**final '-y' changes to '-i'**
tall → taller	attractive → less attractive	greasy → greasier
short → shorter	serious → less serious	healthy → healthier
		busy → busier

It's also very common to use 'not as ~ as' when making negative comparisons:
ex. Korean restaurants are not as expensive as Western restaurants.

What Do You Want for Dinner?

You and your partner are hungry. Using the dialog on the previous page as a model, decide what you'd like to have for dinner. Use the comparatives, and the adjectives from the vocabulary section.

Thai Food

Main Course
Noodles with Beef

Side Dishes
Steamed Vegetables

Drinks
Mango Juice

Dessert
Fruit Plate

Mexican Food

Main Course
Beef or Chicken Burritos

Side Dishes
Cooked Beans

Drinks
Corona Beer

Dessert
Ice Cream

German Food

Main Course
Pork Cutlet

Side Dishes
Mashed Potatoes

Drinks
German Beer

Dessert
Chocolate Cake

Food Bingo

1. Write your opinion under each food. Use the adjectives we've learned.
2. Ask your classmates their opinions and write their opinions in the second blank. Ask one question per student.
3. The first person to get four in a row with DIFFERENT opinion adjectives is the winner. For bingo, only your classmates' opinions count! Your opinions are only written for practice.

A *What do you think of spaghetti?*   **B** *It's delicious.*

Chocolate	Pizza	Chinese Food	Beer
A: _____	A: _____	A: _____	A: _____
B: _____	B: _____	B: _____	B: _____
Jajangmyeon	Steak	Tteokbokki	Ramen
A: _____	A: _____	A: _____	A: _____
B: _____	B: _____	B: _____	B: _____
Sushi	Spaghetti	Coca-Cola	Bulgogi
A: _____	A: _____	A: _____	A: _____
B: _____	B: _____	B: _____	B: _____
Boshintang	Fried Chicken	Cooked Salmon	Fast Food
A: _____	A: _____	A: _____	A: _____
B: _____	B: _____	B: _____	B: _____

Listening Activity

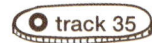 track 35

A Listen to the conversation between Dave and Lisa and fill in the chart.

- Which foods does Dave suggest and why?
- What does Lisa think about his suggestions?

	Dave		Lisa	
	Suggests	Reason	Agrees/Disagrees	Reason
①				
②				

B Listen to the conversation between John and Sylvia and answer the questions. track 36

1 What does Sylvia first suggest for dinner?

2 How does John describe Sylvia's first choice?

3 Why doesn't John want to eat a salad?

4 What kind of food will Sylvia order?

5 How does Sylvia describe jajangmyeon?

Common Mistakes!

Change the Konglish expressions to English ones.

1 I like to *eat* beer. → I like to _____ beer.

2 Too much makkoli makes me *overeat*. → Too much makkoli makes me _____.

3 This appetizer is *service*. → This appetizer is _____.

4 Get some milk at the *super*. → Get some milk at the _____.

5 No thanks, I already have *much* beer. → No thanks, I already have _____ beer.

6 I'll have *cider* please. → I'll have _____ please.

7 Please bring me the *omurice*. → Please bring me the _____.

8 He's a good *cooker*. → He's a good _____.

9 One *shot*! → _____!

Writing Activity — Making Comparisons

Choose five of the topics below. Then write comparative sentences.

Popcorn is saltier than tteokbokki.

- you **vs.** your best friend
- high school **vs.** college
- action movies **vs.** romantic movies
- soju **vs.** beer
- your old boy/girlfriend **vs.** your new one
- pizza **vs.** bindaettok
- Seoul **vs.** Busan
- home cooking **vs.** eating out
- North Korea **vs.** South Korea
- motorcycle **vs.** car

1 _____

2 _____

3 _____

4 _____

5 _____

Wrap-it-up Questions

Get into groups of four. Turn to 'Wrap-it-up Questions' in the back. Students should ONLY look at their own questions.

UNIT 10 Shopping and Fashion

In this unit, you will learn how to:
- describe clothing
- use demonstratives
- talk about prices

Starter   What Are You Wearing Today?

A What are you wearing today? What is your partner wearing? Fill out the boxes below.

> A *What are you wearing?*
>
> B *I'm wearing a green shirt I bought last year.*

	You	Your partner
Head		
Body		
Legs		
Feet		

NOTE
While Korean uses different words to describe putting on or wearing, a ring, a shirt, or shoes, English just uses *put on* and *wear* for nearly all clothing.

B Answer the questions.

1 **Dress Up / Dress Down**

1) Who's the most formally-dressed person in the class?

2) Who's the most casually-dressed person in the class?

3) Who's the most fashionably dressed person in the class?

2 **Accessories**

1) How many people are wearing watches?

2) Does anyone have a hat on?

3) How many people are wearing glasses?

Vocabulary

A Match the pictures with the proper names.

a jeans	b high heels
c suit	d (hiking) boots
e earrings	f coat
g (baseball) cap	h men's underwear
i business shirt	j turtleneck (shirt)
k scarf	l pajamas
m gloves	n sneakers
o jacket	p shorts
q swimming suit	r panties
s sweater	t underwear

B Go over the pictures and pronunciation of the expressions below with your teacher. Please ask questions if you're not sure about something!

C Choose the right word to complete each compliment.

1. I like your earrings. (It, They) look nice on you.
2. I like your tie. (It, They) goes well with your shirt.
3. (That's, Those are) a beautiful dress.
4. (That's, Those are) nice shoes/pants.

UNIT 10 Shopping and Fashion

Conversation 1 — Going Shopping

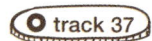

Listen and practice with a partner.

Jason: Wow! Look at this suit! **What do you think**[1]?

Tamara: Are you kidding? A purple, silk suit?

Jason: Well, I guess it is a little **loud**[2], but what's wrong with that?

Tamara: You're getting a new suit for a job interview. Bright purple **isn't the way to go**[3].

Jason: I guess you're right. I was trying to save some money. Normal suits are 300,000 won, the purple one was **on sale for**[4] 125,000.

1 How do you like it | What are your thoughts | Any thoughts
2 flashy | blingy | wild
3 is a bad idea | is a bad choice | is crazy
4 discounted to | reduced to | cut to

Grammar Points — Demonstratives

When talking about something that is close, we use 'this' or 'these'. When talking about something further away, we use 'that' or 'those'. We use 'one' or 'ones' to talk about specific items for the first time. On second reference, we use 'it'.

	Near	Not close
Singular	1. I like this one. I think I'll take it.	3. That one is very pretty. How much is it?
Plural	2. These are cheap. They're only 20,000 won.	4. Those are really expensive. They're more than 100,000 won!

Choose the right word.

1 A: I like that (it, one).

2 B: You mean the red (it, one)?

3 A: No, the one with 'Michigan' printed on the front of (it, one).

84 Speaking for Everyday Life 1

Practice | Saying Numbers

A Practice reading these numbers out loud with a partner and your teacher.

> 2,367   34,000   392,239   104,000   4,972,039   57,000   2015

B Now think of two numbers and write them below. Don't show your partner! Read the numbers to each other, write them down, and check!

You 1 _____   Your Partner 1 _____

     2 _____   2 _____

Activity | Clothes Shopping on a Budget

Two of your family members are having birthdays soon and you have 200,000 won to spend. What will you get them? Tell a partner what you decided to buy and why.

I chose a silk scarf and a denim jacket because...

₩82,000
brand name running shoes

₩45,000
no-name brand running shoes

₩48,000
silk scarf

₩25,000
cotton scarf

₩53,000
silk business shirt

₩17,000
polyester business shirt

₩106,000
high heels

₩125,000
ladies boots

₩126,000
pearl necklace

₩87,000
gold necklace

₩142,000
leather jacket

₩91,000
denim jacket

Conversation 2 — Duty Free Shop

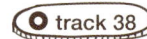

Listen and practice with a partner.

Salesperson: May I help you[1]?

Jong-hee: I came in to get some new boots. I see you have some for $500, but what's that[2] in won?

Salesperson: It's about 500,000 won.

Jong-hee: Ouch! That's a little high[3].

Salesperson: Some of them are on sale for half off[4]. If you let me know which ones you like, I can see if they're on sale.

Jong-hee: I like these leather ones here, and those black suede ones over there.

1 Can I help you | How can I help you | Would you like some help
2 how much is that | what's the price | what's that cost
3 too much for me | more than I wanted to spend | crazy!
4 half price | 50% off

Activity — Using Different Currencies

Listen and practice with a partner.

Getting Prices in Won/Dollars

How much is that in won / dollars?
→ It's ... (in) won/dollars.

How much would that be in won / dollars?
→ That'd be ... (in) won / dollars.

Money Exchange

I'd like to get / buy 1,000 U.S. Dollars / Euros.

What's the exchange rate for U.S. Dollars / Euros / Yen?

With a partner, ask and answer how much the items below are in BOTH won and dollars. (Student A turns to page 109, Student B to 110 for the price information.) To get the price in dollars, just use 1,000 won to 1 dollar.

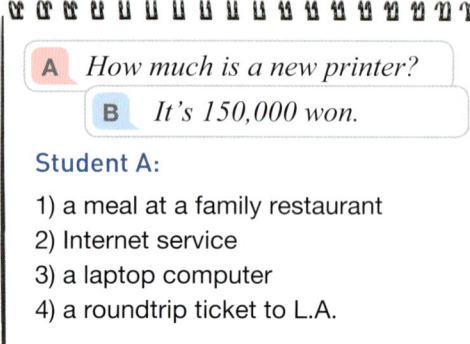

A *How much is a new printer?*
B *It's 150,000 won.*

Student A:
1) a meal at a family restaurant
2) Internet service
3) a laptop computer
4) a roundtrip ticket to L.A.

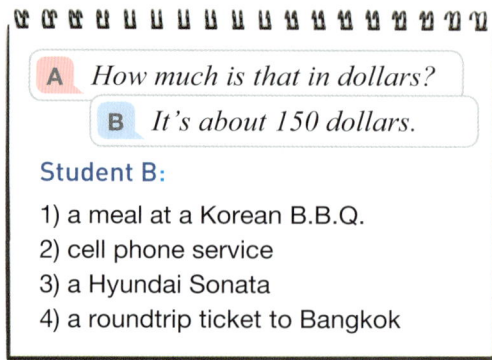

A *How much is that in dollars?*
B *It's about 150 dollars.*

Student B:
1) a meal at a Korean B.B.Q.
2) cell phone service
3) a Hyundai Sonata
4) a roundtrip ticket to Bangkok

 **Street Fashion**

With a partner, read the questions below, then make your own answers.

1. A: Wow, great shirt! Where did you get it?
   B: *I bought it in a second-hand store.*

2. A: Do you mind if I ask how much it cost?
   B: *It only cost 15,000 won. It was a real bargain.*

3. A: Is it made of denim?
   B: *No, it's a cotton / polyester blend.*

4. A: Who made it?
   B: *It's made by a local designer.*

 **Fashion Show**

A. Get into groups of four. Choose two people as 'clothing models' and write down an announcement like the one below.

> Jin-young is dressed casually today. She is wearing white sneakers. They are a no-name brand. She bought them for 28,000 won. Her jeans are by Levi's. They cost 120,000 won. Her white blouse by Polo costs 65,000 won. Finally, she is wearing a gold necklace that costs 36,000 won. She looks very fashionable!

Be sure to include:
1) the kinds of clothes each person is wearing
2) where he/she bought the clothes
3) how much the clothes cost
4) a favorable opinion of the clothes

Model 1: _____

_____

Model 2: _____

_____

B. Now get together with another group and have a mini-fashion show. One person reads while another student models the clothes.

track 39

A **Listen and fill in the blanks.**

> Kate: That's a great looking _____. You should get it.
> William: I don't know. It makes me look bald.
> Kate: You are bald. But the _____ makes you look great. Plus, it matches your _____.
> William: What about the _____ over there?
> Kate: That one? No way. A _____ _____ would be way too warm.
> William: It's only _____ though. I might get both.

track 40

B **Listen and answer the questions.**

1 What does Kate want to buy? _____
2 Does Kate want to wear a new one or an old one? _____
3 Does Kate plan to shop online? _____
4 Does William want to go shopping with Kate? _____
5 Who might Kate go shopping with? _____

Common Mistakes!

Change the Konglish expressions to English ones.

1 That's a great *Y-shirt*. → That's a great _____.
2 She wore a *two-piece* to the party. → She wore a _____ to the party.
3 My brother wears blue *panties*. → My brother wears blue _____.
4 She wore a *one-piece* to the dance. → She wore a _____ to the dance.
5 I like to wear *short pants* in the summer. → I like to wear _____ in the summer.
6 I like *maker* clothes. → I like _____ clothes.
7 Put on your *training wear*. → Put on your _____.
8 That's a warm *pola shirt*. → That's a warm _____.
9 He *wears* his clothes in the morning. → He _____ his clothes in the morning.
10 That's a nice *green color* suit. → That's a nice _____ suit.

Writing Activity — *Clothes for Your Special Day*

Imagine that you will have very special day in your life and write down what you want to wear on that day. It can be the day for your wedding, Christmas Party, or graduation, etc.

- What day is it?
- What will be the weather?
- What kind of clothes do you want to wear?
- What is the style?
- What color is it?

Wrap-it-up Questions

Get into groups of four. Turn to 'Wrap-it-up Questions' in the back. Students should ONLY look at their own questions

UNIT **10** Shopping and Fashion

UNIT 11
Weather and Seasons

In this unit, you will learn how to:
- describe the weather
- talk about different seasons
- answer 'how often' questions

Starter
Weather and Seasons

A With a partner, look at the pictures and ask/answer the questions.

What's the weather like? / How's the weather?

1 It's _____
2 It's _____
3 It's _____
4 It's _____

B With a partner, ask each other what your favorite season is and why.

 What's your favorite season?

 I like _____ the most because _____.

90 Speaking for Everyday Life 1

Vocabulary

A Put the words in the blanks below.

> humid / muggy   rainy / monsoon season   Celsius   clear
> temperature   forecast / report   Fahrenheit   cloudy / overcast

1. People in Korea and most other countries use _____ to say how warm or cold it is. However, Americans still use _____ to talk about the temperature.

2. If there are no clouds in the sky, we say that it is _____.

3. In the summer, when people sweat and the air seems wet, we say that it is very _____.

4. When you want to know if you should wear pants and a warm jacket, or shorts and a t-shirt, you can say, "What is the _____ today?"

5. Between spring and summer, when it rains a lot, you can say it is the _____.

6. The weather _____ tells us what the weather will be like in the future.

7. When we can't see the sun, or blue sky, during the day, we say that it is _____.

B Ask and answer the questions with a partner.

Q: What's the weather like in January / April / July / October?
A: <u>It / The weather is</u>   great / beautiful / nice.
                           sunny / clear
                           terrible
                           cloudy / overcast / gray
                           rainy / snowy / foggy
                           warm / hot
                           cool / cold / freezing

Q: What will the weather be like this weekend?
A: <u>It will</u>   rain / snow.
             clear up / become sunny
             turn cold / cool / warm / hot
             let up / stop soon (when talking about rain)
             cool off / warm up

Conversation 1 — Rainy Summer

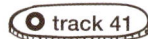 track 41

Listen and practice with a partner.

Min-soo: I wonder if it will ever stop raining[1].

Jane: Yes, I can't believe it's been raining for three days straight!

Min-soo: Jan must really be worried.

Jane: Oh right, she's getting married this weekend. Aren't they having an outdoor wedding?

Min-soo: Yes, they are. They wanted to get married in early September because they thought it would be typical fall weather: cool and clear[2].

Jane: Well, it's been unusually rainy all summer. But I don't think it can rain much more. Hopefully, it will clear up[3] by tomorrow.

Min-soo: Let's hope so. It would be terrible if everyone had to bring umbrellas to the wedding.

Jane: Let's check the Internet for this weekend's forecast.

1 pouring | coming down | drizzling
2 clear blue skies and cooler temperatures | crisp, dry air and beautiful clear skies
3 stop | dry up

Practice

First, complete the sentences below. Then discuss your answers with a partner.

A What do you like to do when it's *hot and humid*?

B *When it's hot and humid*, I like to *go to a hotel downtown and hang out by their swimming pool*!

1 When it's hot and humid, I like to _____.

2 When it's snowy, I like to _____.

3 When it's freezing cold outside, I like to _____.

4 When it's rainy, I like to _____.

5 When it's sunny, I like to _____.

Activity | Weather Forecast

A With a partner, ask and answer questions about the weather in both locations using the charts and phrases below.

> What will the weather be like on Friday in *Seoul*?

> The news said it'll *be sunny, with a high of 2 and a low of -3*.

Date / Day	Seoul	Sydney
Feb 12 / Fri	sunny 2°/-3°	partly cloudy 26°/18°
Feb 13 / Sat	overcast / snow 8°/3°	chance of rain showers 23°/17°
Feb 14 / Sun	heavy snow 9°/4°	heavy thunderstorms 25°/17
Feb 15 / Mon	clear / sunny -1°/-5°	cloudy 25°/19°

The forecast said / says	it will rain / clear up / turn hot.
According to the weather report	it will be windy / sunny / bright this afternoon.
	the high will be 25 and the low will be 5.
	it will get up to 25 (degrees) Friday.
	it'll get down to 15 (degrees).
	there's a slight chance of rain on Saturday.
	it's supposed to rain / snow.
	there's a chance of rain / snow.
	it might rain / snow.

B When travelling to the USA, or when talking to Americans, it's important to be aware of Fahrenheit. The easiest way to go from Celsius to Fahrenheit is to double the temperature and add 30. With a partner, change the temperatures below from Celsius to Fahrenheit.

1 25°C → _____ °F
2 5°C → _____ °F
3 2°C → _____ °F

Conversation 2 — Talking about Seasons

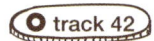 track 42

Listen and practice with a partner.

Paul: What are **winters**[1] like in Korea?

Jin-young: **Winters**[1] are usually **very cold**[2]. It **snows often**[3]. So many people like to **go to resorts for skiing or snowboarding**[4].

Paul: That sounds great. Do you usually do that?

Jin-young: Oh, I never go skiing. How about in your country? Does it **snow often**[3] in **winter**[1]?

Paul: It depends on the region. The southern states are usually warm all year around, but the northern states experience typical seasonal weather.

Situation 1	Situation 2	Situation 3
1 spring	1 fall	1 summer
2 warm but rainy	2 clear and cool	2 hot and humid
3 rains a lot	3 is usually beautiful	3 is normally very muggy
4 see nature come back to life	4 go hiking in the mountains	4 stay inside with the A/C on

Grammar — How Often Questions

A: **How often** do you go skiing in the winter?

B: **Sometimes**.

- always
- usually
- often
- sometimes
- rarely
- never

100%
0%

A: **How often do you** go to the beach in the summer?

B: **Twice a year**.

once	day
twice	week
three times	a month
four times	year

94 Speaking for Everyday Life 1

Activity | What's the Weather Like?

Pretend you and your partner are planning a short trip to the following destinations. Discuss the weather to determine what types of clothing you will take. Also discuss the activities available at each location and ask your partner how often he/she does them.

> Let's go to Vancouver in the winter. What's the weather like?

> It's cold and it rains a lot. We can go skiing in the mountains.

> We'll need to pack heavy winter clothes then.

Sydney
- summer: hot and rarely rainy
- activities: walking tour, boat rides, beach

Washington D.C.
- fall: warm and often clear
- activities: sightseeing, tours, museums

Vancouver
- winter: cold and very rainy
    lots of snow in the mountains
- activities: winter sports in the mountains
    ice skating in the city

Student's Choice
- season / weather: _____
- activities: _____

Pair Work | You Make the Questions!

A Get with a partner and practice the expressions above with the questions below.

1. How often do you wear a swimming suit in summer?
2. How often do you forget your umbrella when it rains?
3. How often do you eat samgyetang or boshingtang in the summer?
4. How often do you go to the countryside to look at the changing leaves in the fall?
5. How often do you go skiing, snowboarding or ice skating in the winter?

B Write down five interesting 'how often' questions below and then practice with a partner.

1. _____
2. _____
3. _____
4. _____
5. _____

Listening Activity

A Listen to the weather report and answer the questions. *track 43*

1. What part of the country will experience freezing temperatures?
   _____

2. Which city will have severe thunderstorms? (California / New Orleans)
   _____

3. Where will the weather be sunny and clear? (New York / California)
   _____

4. Which state will experience the warmest weather? (Arizona / Nevada)
   _____

5. Where will it snow a lot? (New York / Georgia)
   _____

B Listen to the weather report and fill in the blanks. *track 44*

Denver residents should expect _____ streets after midnight from the _____ snowstorm that will drop 6 to 8 centimeters of snow. However, the ice should _____ off by the morning rush hour. The temperature is expected to _____ below freezing around midnight, and that's when the roads will begin _____ over and become dangerous for driving. The snow that falls before then will _____ on the ground but melt on streets. Snowfall amounts will _____ to the west up the Rocky Mountain slope, with Boulder _____ to get heavier snowfalls, up to 12 centimeters. However, most of this snow is expected to melt by Monday with _____ skies and warmer _____.

Common Mistakes!

Change the Konglish expressions to English ones.

1. The sky is very *high* in the fall. → The sky is very _____ in the fall.
2. I need an *aircon* in the summer. → I need an _____ in the summer.
3. Let's *trip* to Jeju-do this fall. → Let's _____ to Jeju-do this fall.
4. Tomorrow, *rain comes*. → _____ tomorrow.
5. I like to *play ski* in the winter. → I like to _____ in the winter.
6. Can you *ride snowboard*? → Can you _____?

Writing Activity — Words for Weather

Put the correct expressions in the weather reports below.

| highs | rain | chance | lows | cloudy |

1. Today's forecast calls for mostly _____ skies with a 50 percent _____ of _____. Today's _____ will be around 30 with _____ in the mid-20s, upper 20s along the coast.

| evening | clouds | chance | rain | sunny |

2. Today's forecast calls for mostly _____ skies with only a 10 percent _____ of rain in the _____. By tomorrow morning, however, the _____ will come in and the chance of _____ goes up to 70 percent.

| low | temperatures | snow | high | freezing |

3. Today's forecast calls for _____ below _____. So dress warm! There is a 60 percent chance of _____ in some areas this afternoon. The _____ today will only reach minus 2, with the _____ going all the way down to minus 10.

| Hurricane | wind | degrees | low | high | scorcher |

4. It looks like a _____ out there today. The _____ will be in the mid-30s and the _____ tonight will only get down to about 30 _____. Tomorrow it should get better though, with a light _____ starting in the morning. The problem is tomorrow night however, when we expect _____ Jennifer to make landfall somewhere along the east coast.

Wrap-it-up Questions

Get into groups of four. Turn to 'Wrap-it-up Questions' in the back of this book. Students should ONLY look at their own questions.

UNIT 12 Sports and Injuries

In this unit, you will learn how to:
- describe various sports
- invite someone to participate in a sport
- describe injuries

Starter — Talking about Sports

A Ask a partner the questions below. Write down his/her answers.

1 Do you like sports? → _____.

2 What kind of sports do you like? → _____.

3 Do you like to play sports? → _____.

4 Are you good at any sports? → _____.

B With a partner, write the questions for the answers below.

1 I'm not much of a sports fan. → *Do you like sports* ?

2 I like soccer the most. → _____ ?

3 I prefer to watch sports. → _____ ?

4 I'm good at tennis. → _____ ?

98 Speaking for Everyday Life 1

Vocabulary

A Write an adjective or short expression under each sport to give your opinion of it.

popular

exciting

B Use the expressions below to describe injuries.

> We use the past tense to describe injuries:
>
> **I broke my leg / sprained my ankle** (while) skiing.*
>
> **I pulled a muscle** (while) lifting weights.
>
> **I hurt my back** (while) playing volleyball.
>
> **I scraped my knees / bruised my arm** (while) rollerblading.
>
> The baseball hit me in the face and gave me **a black eye**.
>
> I fell on my face and **got a bloody nose**.
>
> **I got a bump on my head** after falling off my bike.
>
> It's also common to use 'it' when describing symptoms of pain:
>
> **It's painful** to put weight on my right leg.
>
> **It hurts** when I lift my arm.

NOTE
You can use 'while' to describe the activity you were doing when you were injured, but it's not necessary.

C Ask your partner if he/she was ever injured while playing sports.

A *Did you ever get hurt playing a sport?*

B *Yes, last summer I was rollerblading, when ...*

UNIT **12** Sports and Injuries

Conversation 1 — Yoga Time

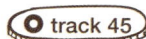

Listen and practice with a partner.

Yu-na: I'm **going skating**[1] later. Do you want to come?

Brian: No way! The last time I tried **skating I almost fell and killed myself**[2]!

Yu-na: What, really?

Brian: Well, not really. I'm just not very good at **skating**[3]. How about **doing some yoga**[4] instead?

Yu-na: I don't know much about **yoga**[5].

Brian: No worries. It's easy and I can help you learn.

Situation 1 – Playing tennis	Situation 2 – Ski time	Situation 3
1 playing tennis	1 going skiing	*Students' choice*
2 tennis I broke a car window with the ball	2 skiing I almost froze to death	
3 tennis	3 skiing	
4 playing golf	4 lifting weights	
5 golf	5 weightlifting	

Grammar Points — Superlatives

A general rule is that if the adjective has less than three syllables, you add '-est' to the end. If the adjective has three or more syllables, you use the word 'most' or 'least' in front of the adjective.

adjective	comparative	superlative
cheap	cheaper	cheapest
cool	cooler	coolest
easy	easier	easiest
silly	sillier	silliest
expensive	more / less expensive	most / least expensive
popular	more / less popular	most / least popular

With a partner, talk about sports. Use superlatives.

A I think golf is the most expensive sport.

B I think American football is the most popular sport in the States..

Activity **Go Fish!**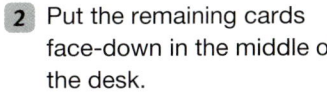

Go Fish with sports. Make groups of four. Your teacher will give you the cards from page 127.

1. Shuffle your deck and deal out six cards to each player.

2. Put the remaining cards face-down in the middle of the desk.

This is the draw pile.

3. Play begins with the person to the left of the dealer.

Start!
dealer

(Before you begin, look at your cards and take out any sets of four.)

5. a. If the student has a matching card, he/she should accept the invitation.

Sure, that sounds exciting.

Tom gives all his tennis cards to A. A continues.

(A continues until someone says "no" to him/her, or he/she runs out of cards.)

4. He/She asks another player if they have a card by inviting that student to do the sport.

Tom, do you want to play tennis?

5. b. If the student doesn't have a matching card, he/she should refuse and give a reason.

A takes a card from the draw pile. A's turn ends. Now it is B's turn.

No thanks. Tennis is boring.

6. Once players have FOUR of the same cards, they should put that set down on the table.*

(When a student runs out of cards, he/she takes another card from the draw pile.)

7. When the draw pile runs out*, play continues until all players have no more cards in their hands.

No cards left!

(If there are no cards left, your turn ends. The next player starts.)

8. The winner is the student with the most sets of cards at the end.

Conversation 2 — Where Does It Hurt?

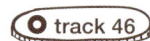

Listen and practice with a partner.

Jake: What's wrong with your hand?

Jill: I **cut it chopping onions last night**[1].

Jake: It looks kind of serious.

Jill: It's fine. **I cleaned it and put on a bandage**[2].

Jake: Still, you might want to get it looked at by a doctor.

> [1] accidently shut a door on it this morning
> | played a lot of tennis yesterday and it gave me blisters
> [2] I took a couple of aspirin and it feels better
> | It happens every spring when I start playing tennis again

Pair Work — What Happened to You?

Look at the pictures. Then unscramble the sentences to make dialogs similar to the one above.

A

____ I messed it up skiing.

_1_ What happened to your leg?

____ No, the doctor took an X-ray and nothing's broken.

____ You didn't break anything?

B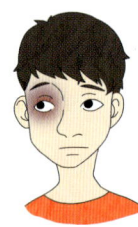

____ No! There was ice on the sidewalk.

____ I tripped and fell. My head hit a step.

____ What's up with your eye?

____ Drinking too much again?

C

____ Somebody in a car hit you?

____ Yes. I was going slow, so it's just cuts and bruises.

____ Ouch! That looks painful. What happened?

____ No, the rain yesterday made the road really slippery and I fell.

____ Are you sure it's not serious?

____ I got into an accident on my bike.

Ouch! What Happened?

Make groups of three. Your teacher will assign you one of the pictures below. Look at your picture – this is you. Make an interesting story about what happened. After everyone makes up a good story, tell your group what happened.

A: I went skiing at Phoenix Park last weekend. I fell and broke my arm and leg. Now I have to wear a cast for six weeks.

Remember to get advice from everyone in your group after you read your story.

B: You should stay home and rest.

C: You should stay off your leg.

1. skinned my elbow
2. fell down and bruised my butt
3. got a black eye
4. lost some teeth
5. hurt my back
6. got a bloody nose
7. smashed my fingers
8. got a bump on my head

UNIT 12 Sports and Injuries

 *Listening Activity*

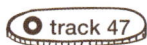 track 47

Listen to the three conversations and fill in the chart for each.

	Sport	Opinion	How often
① Sam			
② Nate			
③ Noah			

Common Mistakes!

Konglish to English	Grammar Points
I like **to do** exercise. (X) → I like **to exercise**. (O) → I like **exercising**. (O) I like **to ride** snowboard. (X) → I like **to snowboard**. (O) → I like **snowboarding**. (O)	*Exercise* and *snowboard* (also *ski*, *skate*, *inline-skate*, etc.) are both nouns and verbs. There is no reason to use the verbs *do*, *ride* or *play* with another verb.
I like **to play** bowling. (X) → I like **to bowl**. (O) → I like **bowling**. (O)	*Play* is used with sport names that are only nouns. (e.g. I like to *play soccer*., I can *play baseball*.) *Golf* is the exception. You can use 'play' with golf. → I like to *golf*. / I like to *play golf*.
My arm **is sick**. (X) → My arm **hurts**. (O)	*Sick* refers to a disease or illness. Your entire body can be sick, but a part of your body cannot be sick. We would usually say *hurt instead*. (e.g. I *hurt* my leg., It *hurts* when I bend my knee.)

Change the Konglish expressions to English ones.

1 I like *to swimming*. → I like _____.

2 Can you *play bowling*? → Can you _____?

3 I like *to skiing*. → I like _____.

4 I can't ski because my leg *is sick*. → I can't ski because my leg _____.

5 I like *to do exercise*. → I like _____.

6 I like *to ride rollerblade*. → I like _____.

104 Speaking for Everyday Life 1

Writing Activity — *Survey Report*

Let's have a survey in the class about the sports below. Find out the most beloved sport in your class and write about the result in a report form.

Which do you like the most among these sports?

Sports	The Number of Person
Soccer	
Speed Skating	
Swimming	
Ice hockey	
Relay	
Rafting	
Bicycle Race	
Figure Skating	
Volley Ball	
Tennis	

Example: According to the survey, 3 of the classmates like swimming and 5 people like tennis. There are also 7 people who like ice hockey and figure skating is the most beloved sport with 12 people. Unfortunately, there is no one that likes rafting.

_____
_____
_____
_____
_____
_____

Wrap-it-up Questions

Get into groups of four. Turn to 'Wrap-it-up Questions' in the back. Students should ONLY look at their own questions.

Appendix

- Activity File
- Listening Script
- Wrap-it-up Questions
- Answers
- Go Fish

Activity File

Unit 02 Activity *Gap Fill*

Look at the chart below. Ask and answer the questions to fill in the missing information.

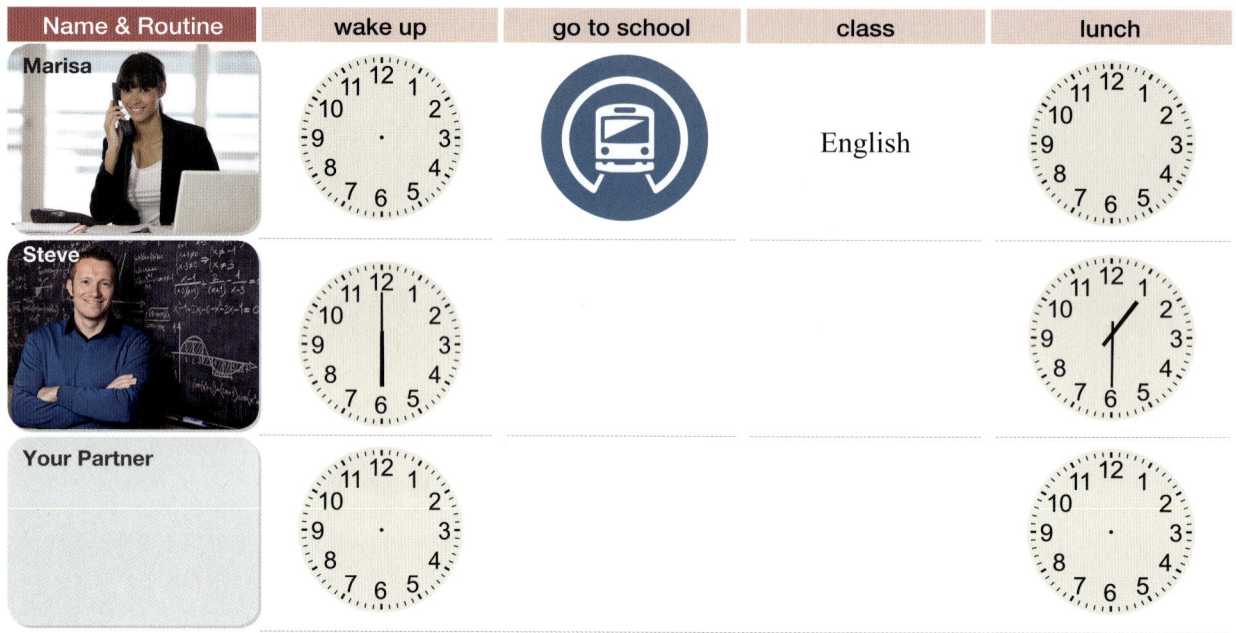

Unit 05 Activity

With a partner, fill in the calendar with these events.

> **Ask A when these events are:**
> - the presentation
> - Sang-kyu's wedding
> - Hyun-ah's birthday
> - the baseball game

[Student B's Calendar]

SUN	MON	TUE	WED	THU	FRI	SAT
	1	2	3	4	5	6
7 *Tae-hun's birthday*	8	9	10	11	12	13
14	15	16	17 *test*	18	19 *the Girl's Gen concert*	20
21	22 ←	23 *school festival*	24 →	25	26	27
28	29	30				

108   Speaking for Everyday Life 1

Activity *Which Exit?*

You have just arrived in a popular place in your city by subway. You are there to meet a friend, but you don't know where he/she is. Call him/her and ask for directions. Your partner should tell you which exit to use.

Your partner wants to meet in these places. Give him/her directions from the subway.

| my apartment | London Coffeeshop | pet store | video game arcade | karaoke |

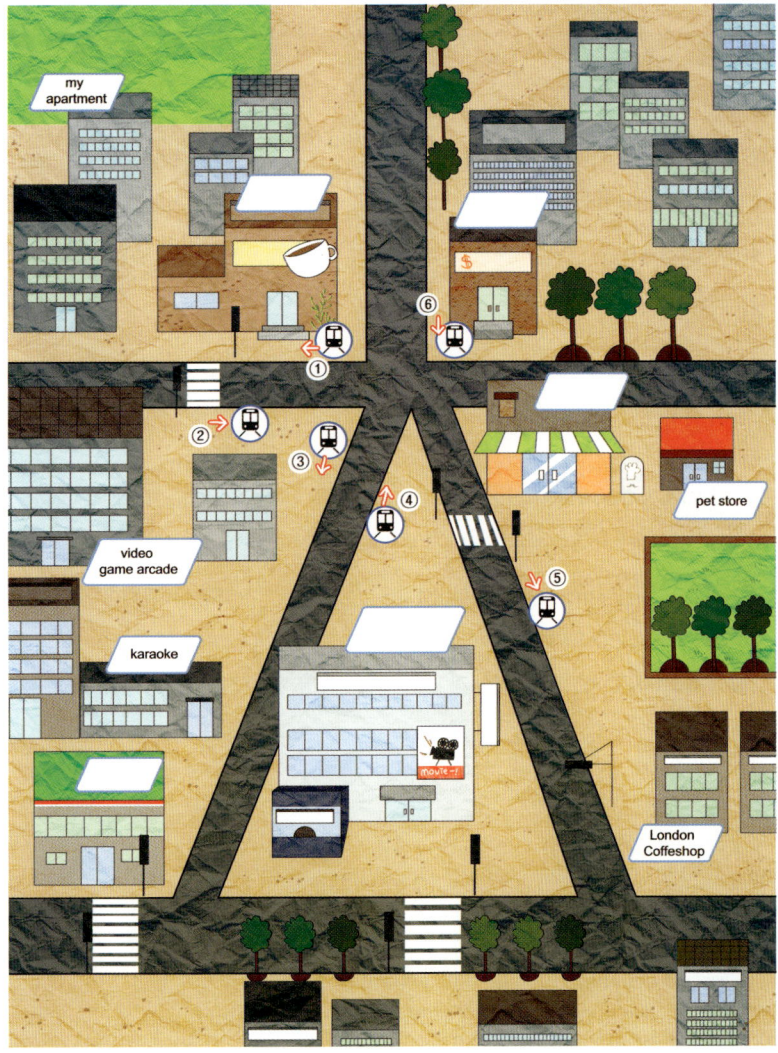

Situation A

The prices Student B wants to know:

1. a meal at a Korean B.B.Q. → 11,000 won
2. cell phone service → 19,000 won (a month)
3. a Hyundai Sonata → 19.5 million won
4. a roundtrip ticket to Bangkok → 450,000 won

Appendix **109**

Unit 08 Activity Student Resumes

Tom Jones

Education	Hongik University	expected February 2014
	- B.A. in Art and Design	
Experience	Architects and Interiors	Jan. 2012 - present
	- help design room interiors for houses and offices	
	- help with customer service	

Choi Jin-hyuk

Education	Busan National University	expected February 2014
	- B.S. in Business and Marketing	
Experience	Kim's Kimbap	May. 2012 – Dec. 2012
	- took customer orders	
	- helped make 10 different kinds of kimbap	

Bak Sun-hye

Education	National Education University	expected February 2014
	- Elementary Education Bachelor's Degree	
Experience	Chongno Elementary School #5	Sep. 2013 - present
	- help licensed teacher teach first-grade students	
	- assist teachers with grading and administration	

Unit 10

Situation B

The prices Student A wants to know:

1. a meal at a family restaurant → 24,000 won
2. Internet service → 31,000 won (a month)
3. a laptop computer → 1.2 million won
4. a roundtrip ticket to LA → 800,000 won

Practice *Short Phone Conversations*

With a partner, read the dialogs and fill in the blanks. Then answer the questions.

Reserving a Table at a Restaurant

You are the head waiter at Drago's restaurant in New Orleans. A person is calling to reserve a table. You need to know the name for the reservation and the number of people in the group. It's important to confirm information when conducting a telephone call for business.

You:	Drago's in New Orleans. How may I help you?
Customer:	_____.
You:	Let me check. I'm sorry, we are fully booked at 7. However, there are tables available at 8 p.m.
Customer:	_____.
You:	And how many people will be in your party?
Customer:	_____.
You:	Okay, that's a party of five under the name of Dunaway at 8 p.m.
Customer:	_____.

- When does the customer originally want the reservation?
- What is the name for the reservation?
- How many people are in the group?

Texting and Calling a Friend

You are trying to call your friend, but his/her phone seems to be off. You text him/her instead. You want to meet him/her for dinner next week.

Your Friend:	(text) _____.
You:	(text) I'm in Japan. Turned off roaming. Call me on Cacao.
You:	(answering phone) Hello.
Your Friend:	_____.
You:	Yes, I'm here on business. I'll be back in Seoul Thursday afternoon.
Your Friend:	_____.
You:	Sounds great. I'll call you when I get back to set up a time.

- What question does your friend text you?
- Why is your friend calling?
- What kind of food does your friend want to eat?

Appendix **111**

Listening Script

Unit 01

Dialog A

Terry: Hi, I'm Terry.

Su-jin: Hi Terry, I'm Su-jin. Nice to meet you.

Terry: Same here. Do you go to UCLA?

Su-jin: No, I'm visiting a friend here. I'm a student at a university in Seoul, Korea.

Terry: Oh, I'm in my last year at UCLA. I'm studying biology.

Su-jin: What a coincidence! I'm studying biology too! But I'm a freshman.

Dialog B

Su-jin: Terry, I'd like you to meet my best friend, Min-jeong. Min-jeong, this is Terry. He's studying biology, like me!

Min-jeong: Wow, that's cool. Nice to meet you Terry.

Terry: Same here. What are you majoring in?

Min-jeong: Business Management. I just started this year.

Su-jin: Min-jeong and I went to the same high school in Korea. How about you, Terry? Where are you from?

Terry: I'm from Sydney, Australia.

Unit 02

Dialog A

Eun-mi: You look tired. What time did you get home last night?

Hyun-ah: I got home at 11:15. What time did you get off work?

Eun-mi: I got off work at 9:40. And then took the subway at 10:30.

Hyun-ah: Why were you out so late?

Eun-mi: I had too much work.

Dialog B

Ed: Did you text me at 4:00 a.m. this morning?

Sally: Yeah, sorry. I was up studying until 4:30 and had a question.

Ed: Sorry, I didn't even hear my phone. I went to sleep early, at around nine, and didn't wake up until after eight.

Sally: Wow, you slept for almost 12 hours? Are you okay?

Ed: I was sick for two or three days, but I'm better now.

Unit 03

Dialog A

1. Excuse me, sorry to bother you. Would you happen to know if there is a bank near here?

2. Hey, where's gate number 68?

3. Hi, could you tell me where the cereal is?

Dialog B

Ralph: Hi, Could you tell me how to get into town from here?

Information Clerk: Sure. The fastest way is by taxi. There's a taxi stand just outside the doors to your right. Cross the street and there will be a line of taxis to your left. Please remember there is usually a line of people waiting, so don't cut in front and grab the first taxi you see! Or you could take a bus, which is a lot cheaper.

Ralph: Yeah, I think I'll take the bus. Where can I catch one to downtown? I'm staying at the Pilton Hotel.

Information Clerk: You should take bus 1006. Go out the same doors, but don't cross the street. Instead, turn right and walk down the sidewalk about 20 meters. You will see a sign for bus stop number 2. Bus 1006 stops there.

Ralph: Great, thanks. One more question. Could you tell me where I can change some money?

Information Clerk: Yes, there's a bank across the lobby from here. It's between the escalator and the elevator.

Ralph: Oh, okay, I see the sign. Thanks!

Unit 04

Dialog A

Kathy: Do you like to exercise?

Al: Sure. I like to do yoga and hike. How about you?

Kathy: I love to ski on weekends. I also enjoy martial arts.

Al: I like to ski too! Maybe we can go together sometime.

Dialog B

Kathy: That sounds great. A group of us are going skiing next weekend. Do you want to come?

Al: I've got a cooking class that weekend. How about a different weekend?

Kathy: Sure, I'll let you know the next time we go.

Unit 05

Dialog A

Son: Mom, Dad was born in 1971, right?

Mom: No, he was born in 1970, April 6th.

Son: Oh, I knew the day, I just wasn't sure of the year. How about Grandpa—Dad's father?

Mom: Let me look it up. He was born on Jan 13th, 1943. Why are you so interested in birthdays?

Son: I'm putting important dates in my smart phone to remind me.

Mom: That's a good idea. Do you need me to tell you my birthdate?

Son: No, of course I remember yours, Mom!

Dialog B

Mom: Are there any other birthdates you want to know?

Son: Yes, can you tell me the birthdays for Grandma and Granny?

Mom: Well, Grandma was born on March 10th, 1952.

Son: Ok, got it. And Granny?

Mom: Let's see. She was born on Jan. 15th, 1948.

Son: Ok, thanks Mom. Now I have everyone's birthday.

Mom: Good—now you won't forget to send birthday cards!

Unit 06

Nolan: A guy I know is really looking to meet someone. Would you be interested?

Jackie: What's he like?

Nolan: Sam's average-height but really fit. A lot of women say he's cute.

Jackie: Not bad, but what's he really like?

Nolan: Well, he can be a little wild, but he's also outgoing and really nice.

Jackie: My friend Susan, the super pretty girl you met last year, is looking to date again.

Nolan: Really? The tall one, with long hair?

Jackie: Yep, that's her.

Nolan: Oh wow, that'd be great. Anything I should know about her?

Jackie: She's really stubborn, kind of moody, and not that smart.

Nolan: No problem. She sounds great.

Unit 07

Dialog A

Man: Ace Auto Repairs. How may I help you?

Woman: Can I speak to Ben, please?

Man: I'm sorry, he's on his lunch break now. Can I take a message?

Woman: Do you know what time he'll be back?

Man: He should be back at 2 p.m.

Woman: My name is Alice Stenbeck. Ben left a message for me earlier about replacing the car battery. Tell him to go ahead and do it.

Man: Ok, I will tell him to put a new car battery in your car.

Woman: Thank you. Also, when will my car be ready?

Man: You can pick it up at 5 p.m.

Woman: Ok, thank you.

Man: Thanks for calling Ace Auto Repairs.

Unit 08

Dialog A

Interviewer: Nice to meet you. Please have a seat and we'll get started. The first part of the interview will be in English.

Tae-ho: Nice to meet you, too. I have an extra copy of my résumé in English in case you need it.

Interviewer: No problem. I've been looking it over and I'm curious about your work history. You've only had part-time jobs?

Tae-ho: Yes, I worked part-time during the school year, more during summer and winter vacations.

Dialog B

Interviewer: I'd like to see more experience for this position.

Tae-ho: Ma'am, I have great grades, reference letters from a professor and a former boss, and I learn fast. I'll quickly become a strong part of your team.

Interviewer: Ok, good positive answer. I'll check your references. Next question … why do you want to work for us?

Tae-ho: This job is exactly what I've been looking for. It matches my major, my part-time work, and I'm really interested in the field.

Unit 09

Dialog A

Dave: I'm hungry. Let's get an appetizer. How about crab cakes?

Lisa: Really? They are way more expensive than any of the other appetizers.

Dave: Ok, then how about getting chicken wings? They are less expensive and very tasty.

Lisa: Let's get the spring rolls. They aren't as greasy as the chicken wings and they are healthier than anything else.

Dave: You know, before you started your diet, it was more fun going out to dinner with you.

Dialog B

Sylvia: John, what do you think about getting curry tonight?

John: Curry is too spicy. How about steaks? They are more filling.

Sylvia: I'm not that hungry. How about getting a couple of large Caesar salads?

John: No, I need something tastier and more filling.

Sylvia: Let's get Chinese food. I can order something light and healthy, and you can get something more fattening.

John: Very funny. But Jajangmyeon sounds good.

Sylvia: Ugh! Jajangmyeon is too salty if you ask me.

Unit 10

Dialog A

Kate: That's a great looking hat. You should get it.

William: I don't know. It makes me look bald.

Kate: You are bald. But the hat makes you look great. Plus, it matches your jacket.

William: What about the one over there?

Kate: That one? No way. A leather hat would be way too warm.

William: It's only $45 though. I might get both.

Dialog B

Kate: I need a new dress for the party next week.

William: What's wrong with all of the dresses you have now?

Kate: Nothing is wrong with them; I just need a new one. It's a special party.

William: Off the rack or do you want something special?

Kate: I was planning on trying those new boutiques downtown. Some of those designers are fantastic.

William: As long as you go with your sister and not me, no problem.

Unit 11

Dialog A

And now for a look at the weather across the country. Arctic air continues to flow down into the eastern part of the country, bringing freezing temperatures from Maine down south to the Carolinas. New York should expect heavy snowfall over the weekend. Showers and thunderstorms are expected along the Gulf Coast states with severe thunderstorms predicted for New Orleans. Rain is also forecast for the Northwest, with heavy rain expected in Seattle. Further south, sunny and clear skies are expected over much of California and into the Southwest. Arizona will be the warmest state over the weekend, with temperatures ranging from 20 to 22 degrees Celsius.

Dialog B

Denver residents should expect icy streets after midnight from the overnight snowstorm that will drop 6 to 8 centimeters of snow. However, the ice should melt off by the morning rush hour. The temperature is expected to drop below freezing around midnight, and that's when the roads will begin icing over and become dangerous for driving. The snow that falls before then will stick on the ground but melt on streets. Snowfall amounts will increase to the west up the Rocky Mountain slope, with Boulder expected to get heavier snowfalls, up to 12 centimeters. However, most of this snow is expected to melt by Monday with sunny skies and warmer temperatures.

Unit 12

Sam: I'm going to go workout this morning. Do you want to come?

Whitney: Do you workout every morning?

Sam: Yep, I try to. I love a good workout; it wakes me up in the morning.

Whitney: Well, have fun. I'm going back to sleep.

Terri: You're going golfing?

Nate: Yeah, I hate it, but I have to do it for business.

Terri: Wow, I didn't know you knew how to golf. How often do you go?

Nate: Once or twice a year.

Britney: I just started a new taekwondo class. You want to come?

Noah: I already do taekwondo 2-3 times a week. I've done it for years.

Britney: I didn't know that. Are you any good?

Noah: I like doing it, but I'm still not that good. It takes a long time to master.

Wrap-it-up questions

Student One

UNIT 01
- Do you like meeting new people? Why or why not?
- Do you have many close friends?
- Do you have any friends from another country? What country? What language do you use with them?

UNIT 02
- What time do you get up on school days? How about on weekends?
- What's the first thing you do after getting up?
- How do you spend your weekends? How about your evenings on weekdays?

UNIT 03
- Did a foreigner ever ask you for directions in Korea?
- Use the expressions learned in this unit to ask one of your partners if there are any landmarks (well-known, easy-to-find places) near his or her house. If so, ask that person how to get there from his/her house.

UNIT 04
- Do you have any hobbies?
- Is there a new hobby you want to learn? What is it?
- What's an exciting hobby? What's a boring hobby? What's a dangerous hobby?

UNIT 05
- When is your birthday? Do you do anything special that day? Do you eat anything special for breakfast?
- Do you do anything special for your mother/father's birthday? How about your boy/girlfriend's birthday?
- What is your favorite holiday?

UNIT 06
- Who's the best-looking person you know among your friends or relatives? Why do you think so? Describe her/him.
- Describe your favorite movie star (appearance and personality).
- Did you look different when you were younger? How?

UNIT 07
- What's your favorite season? Why? What do you do?
- Do you like rainy days? Why (Why not)?
- Some people think snowy days are romantic. Do you? Why (Why not)?

UNIT 08
- Did you ever have a part-time job, or a summer job? What did you do? Did you like it?
- Did you ever have a job interview? How was it?
- What kind of job do you want? Is it close to your major?

| UNIT 09 | • What do you usually have for dinner? Do you like it?
• What's the best meal your mom has ever cooked?
• How would you describe the differences between Korean and Japanese or Chinese food? |
|---|---|
| UNIT 10 | • Where's the best place to buy electronics?
• What's the most expensive item of clothing you own? Where did you get it?
• How much do you spend in a typical month? What do you usually spend your money on? |
| UNIT 11 | • How often do you use your cell phone? Who do you usually talk to?
• How often do you send text messages? Do you ever send them in English?
• Is your phone bill high every month? |
| UNIT 12 | • Do you do anything to stay in shape? What is it?
• What's the most boring sport you've ever played?
• Did you ever injure yourself playing a sport? What happened? |

Student Two

| UNIT 01 | • Do you want a friend from another country? Why or why not?
• Do you like studying English? Why or why not?
• Do you like your major? Why or why not? What major do you like? |
|---|---|
| UNIT 02 | • What's the last thing you do before you go to sleep?
• Do you usually take a shower in the morning or the evening?
• Are you a morning person or a night person? |
| UNIT 03 | • How would you feel if someone asked you for directions in English? What would you do?
• Use the expressions learned in this unit to ask one of your partners if there is a bathroom near the classroom. If so, ask for directions. |
| UNIT 04 | • What is your father's hobby? What is your mother's hobby?
• What is an expensive hobby? What is a cheap hobby?
• Which hobby sounds better to you – painting, scuba diving or yoga? Why? |
| UNIT 05 | • What do you usually do on Christmas? Chuseok? Lunar New Year? Valentine's Day? The first day of summer ('Chobok')?
• What dates are important in your family (birthdays, anniversaries, etc.)? What do you do on those days? |

- Do you do anything special on the anniversary of the death of an ancestor (e.g. your grandfather)?

UNIT 06
- Who's the worst-looking entertainer in Korea? Why do you think so?
- Who do you resemble the most in your family?
- What is your ideal boyfriend/girlfriend like (appearance and personality)?

UNIT 07
- How often do you go on a date?
- How often do you drink?
- How often do you exercise?

UNIT 08
- Are you a hard worker? How do you know?
- Do you like to work alone or be part of a team?
- Can you get along well with a boss? Your co-workers? Can you be a good boss?

UNIT 09
- Do you eat a lot of or very little junk food? Is there any reason for this?
- Can you cook anything? What is it? How do you cook it?
- What's your favorite dish? Describe it. Why do you like it?

UNIT 10
- Do you ever shop in department stores? Which ones?
- What's the most expensive thing you purchased recently? Describe it.
- Where do you shop for clothes?

UNIT 11
- Do you ever call overseas? Who do you call? Is it expensive?
- Do you use your cell phone on the bus or subway?
- Did you ever forget to turn off your phone in a movie and get a call? What happened?

UNIT 12
- What's the most expensive sport you've ever participated in?
- Would you rather watch sports or play sports?
- What's the most popular sport in Korea these days?

Student Three

UNIT 01
- Where are you from? Where do you live now?
- What year are you in?
- Do you want to go to grad (graduate) school someday? Why or why not?

UNIT 02
- How do you get to school? How much time does it take?
- Do you play computer games? When? For how long?
- Do you have a part-time job? When? What do you do? Do you like it?

UNIT 03	• Have you ever been lost? • Use the expressions learned in this unit to ask one of your partners if there is a good restaurant near your school. If so, ask for directions.
UNIT 04	• Which hobby sounds better to you – bowling, playing cards (go-stop, poker, etc.) or golf? Why? • Are there hobbies that are mainly for men? What are they? • Are there hobbies mainly for women? What are they?
UNIT 05	• How big is your family? • On holidays do you usually visit your father's family or mother's family? Or does everyone visit your home? • Is divorce common in Korea? If someone is divorced, (or their parents are divorced), do they try to keep it a secret, or is it common to talk about?
UNIT 06	• Is your personality more like your mother's or your father's? Are you happy about it? • Where is a good place to go on a date? Why? • Is there anything you'd like to change about your appearance? What is it?
UNIT 07	• What's the best food to eat during the summer? Winter? • Where's the best place to go on vacation in the summer? Winter? • Where's the best place to enjoy the fall colors?
UNIT 08	• What's the most important thing for you when you choose a job? Salary? Company? Fun/Interesting people to work with? Vacation? • Do you want to work in a foreign country someday? For how long? How about an overseas business trip – does that sound like fun or just a lot of stress? • Is it OK for women to work after they get married? How about after they have children?
UNIT 09	• Compare samgyupsal, boshintang and hway (raw fish). • What's your favorite restaurant? Why? Where is it? • Do you like bondaegi? Have you ever tried it?
UNIT 10	• If you suddenly got 500,000 won, what would you do with it? • What is the most expensive gift you have ever received? • How often do you shop online? What do you buy? What site(s) do you prefer?
UNIT 11	• Do you use your phone in class? How often? Did you ever get in trouble for that? • Do you have your own homepage? What's the address? Does it look good? • How often do you use the Internet? What do you do? What are your favorite websites?

UNIT 12
- What do you think is the most dangerous sport in the world?
- When was the last time you hurt yourself? What happened?
- What is your favorite sports team?

Student Four

UNIT 01
- Do you shake hands when you meet someone new? Bow?
- What's a good major to get a job? Bad major?
- Is it easy to change majors?

UNIT 02
- What time is it (now)?
- Do you have any hobbies that you do on certain days at certain times?
  (yoga, cooking, working on your homepage, etc.)
- When and where do you have lunch? Who do you have lunch with?

UNIT 03
- When was the last time you asked for directions? Where were you going?
- Use the expressions learned in this unit to ask one of your partners if there is a convenience store near your school. If so, ask for directions.

UNIT 04
- What is the strangest hobby you can think of?
- Do you want the same hobby as your boy/girlfriend or do you prefer your own hobby?
- In the United States a common hobby is shooting a gun at a target, inside or outside. What do you think of this hobby? Is it common in Korea?

UNIT 05
- When you were young, who was your favorite relative? How about now?
- Is anyone in your family not Korean? Do you have any relatives who live overseas?
- Is it OK to marry a non-Korean? What would your family say?

UNIT 06
- Do you like blind dates? What about dating someone you met on the Internet?
- What do you think of plastic surgery?
- Would you ever consider marrying an unattractive person?

UNIT 07
- Do you want to live in a place with no winter, where it's always warm?
- How do you keep cool in the summer?
- How often do you watch the weather forecast?

UNIT 08
- Are you good at job interviews? Do they give you a lot of stress?
- What can you do to prepare for a job interview?

• Is it hard to find a good job? What can you do to find one?

UNIT 09
• What traditional Korean foods are healthy?
• What is the most disgusting food you have ever eaten? Describe it.
• What do you think about eating raw fish? How about raw octopus or squid?

UNIT 10
• What is the ideal gift for a boyfriend or girlfriend?
• How much does a new desktop computer cost these days?
• Would you ever pay more than 500,000 won for a piece of clothing?

UNIT 11
• Do you ever use the Internet in English? Why? What sites?
• If you call a wrong number, what do you do?
• Do you get a lot of spam? What do you do about it? How about sales calls – do a lot of salespeople call you? What do you say to them?

UNIT 12
• Do you think sports should be more common in Korean high schools?
• Where is the best place to exercise?
• What's good advice for someone with a broken leg?

Answers

Unit 01

Starter

B 1. What's your name? 2. What's your major?
3. What year are you in? 4. Where are you from?
5. Where do you live?

Vocabulary

A 1. freshman, sophomore 2. senior, junior
3. hometown 4. major

B 1. ⓔ 2. ⓕ 3. ⓑ 4. ⓒ 5. ⓐ 6. ⓚ 7. ⓙ
8. ⓓ 9. ⓗ 10. ⓖ 11. ⓘ

Practice

B 1. Who is your favorite professor?
2. What are you majoring in?
3. Where are you from?
4. When did you start college?
5. Why are you studying history?

Listening Activity

A Nice to meet you, I'm a student, in my last year, biology, a freshman

B 1. False 2. True 3. False 4. False

Common Mistakes

B 1. unemployed 2. a very good student
3. absent 4. class reunion

Unit 02

Starter

A 1. I get up at six. 2. I eat breakfast at seven.
3. I leave home at 7:30. 4. I get to school at 8:15.
5. I study from 9 a.m. to 10 p.m.
6. I go to bed at midnight

B 1. What time do you get up?
2. What time do you take a shower?
3. What time do you eat breakfast?
4. What time do you get to school?
5. What time do you study?
6. What time do you go to bed?

Vocabulary

A 1. noon, midnight 2. leave, get 3. from, to
4. stay up late, sleep in/late
5. get dressed (put on clothes) 6. wake up
7. brush my teeth 8. put on makeup

B 1. at 2. on 3. in 4. in 5. at 6. at 7. in
8. on 9. at

C 1. On, at, from, to 2. in, at 3. Before 4. at
5. from, to

Listening Activity

A 1. 11:15 p.m. 2. 10:30 p.m.
3. 9:40 p.m.

B 1. She texted the man at 4 a.m.
2. She was up studying.
3. He went to bed at around nine.
4. He woke up after eight.
5. He was sick for two or three days.

Common Mistakes

1. for eight hours 2. at 4 p.m. 3. This weekend
4. At, was sleeping 5. go to sleep 6. next Monday
7. get dressed (put on my clothes)

Unit 03

Starter

A 1. Rank 1-street 2. Rank 3-airport
3. Rank 2-supermarket

B 1. Where do you keep the shampoo?
2. Excuse me, could you please tell me where gate 57 is?
3. Would you happen to know where the nearest subway station is?

C 1. ⓖ 2. ⓒ 3. ⓔ 4. ⓑ 5. ⓓ 6. ⓐ 7. ⓕ

Activity

A 1. b 2. a 3. c

Pair work

1. straight ahead 2. just past 3. kitty corner to
4. just before 5. in the middle of the next/second block
6. at the end of the block

Listening Activity

1. e   2. c   3. a

Unit 04
Starter

(A) 1. Do you like hiking? How about going hiking this Sunday?
2. Do you like skiing? How about going skiing this weekend?
3. Do you like playing computer games? How about playing computer games online sometime.
4. Do you like shopping? How about going shopping after class?

Vocabulary

(A) 1. accept   2. turn down   3. reschedule   4. hobby
5. hanging out   6. get together

(B) 1. ⓓ   2. ⓕ   3. ⓖ   4. ⓑ   5. ⓐ   6. ⓗ   7. ⓒ
8. ⓔ   9. ⓚ   10. ⓘ   11. ⓙ   12. ⓛ

Listening Activity

(A) exercise, hike, about, ski, enjoy, ski

(B) 1. Next weekend   2. Yes, she does.
3. He is attending a cooking class.
4. No, not this time. Al will go with Kathy next time.

Common Mistakes

1. sci-fi / science fiction   2. play pool   3. go bowling
4. appointment at 2 p.m.   5. go Dutch for
6. hung out, a   7. bored

Unit 05
Starter

(A) 1. February 14th   2. the fourth Thursday in November
3. December 25th   4. October 31th

Vocabulary

(A) 1. lunar calendar   2. solar calendar
3. day off   4. Valentine's Day
5. Arbor Day   6. April Fool's Day
7. White Day

(B) 1. first   2. second   3. third, of
4. August, fifteenth of August twenty-twenty-one

Activity

(A) 1. R   2. Q   3. N   4. F   5. E   6. L   7. K   8. G
9. H   10. W   11. V   12. C   13. D   14. Z   15. Y
16. M   17. S   18. T   19. P   20. O   21. B
22. A   23. U   24. X

Listening Activity

(A) 1. 1970   2. April 6th   3. 1943   4. January   5. 13th

(B) birthdates, Granny, March 10th, January 15th, forget

Common Mistakes

1. oldest   2. There are five people in my family.   3. my
4. are, plans   5. Actual Name e.x.) James   6. older

Unit 06
Starter

(A) 1. He's kind of thick and short.
2. She's tall and really thin.
3. She's plain looking.
4. He's got red hair and freckles.
5. He's handsome and has short hair.
6. He's chubby.

Practice

(B) 1. What does he/she look like?
2. How tall is he/she?
3. What is his/her first impression?
4. What is his/her personality?

Activity

1. met   2. was washing   3. was waiting   4. did
5. cleaned   6. got   7. said   8. said   9. threw
10. walked   11. was   12. did not have
13. washed   14. moved   15. washed   16. left
17. was working   18. thought   19. laughed
20. decided   21. wanted   22. lived   23. asked
24. knew   25. called   26. asked

Listening Activity

	Appearance	Personality
① Sam	average-height, really fit, cute	a little wild, outgoing, really nice
② Susan	super pretty, tall, long hair	stubborn, kind of moody, not that smart

Unit 07

Vocabulary

Ⓐ 1. caps   2. vibrate   3. caller ID
4. swipe   5. missed   6. mobile

Grammar Point

Ⓐ 1. ⓑ   2. ⓒ   3. ⓐ   4. ⓕ   5. ⓔ   6. ⓓ   7. ⓖ

Pair Work

Ⓐ 1. ⓒ   2. ⓓ   3. ⓑ   4. ⓐ

Ⓑ 1. Could you give me change for a 1,000 won bill?
2. Would you please lend me your laptop?
3. Could you help me to move this weekend?

Listening Activity

Ⓐ ① Ben   ② Ms. Alice Stenbeck   called
③ Tell him to put a new car battery in my car.

Ⓑ 1. Ben
2. Alice Stenbeck
3. Ben's coworker
4. Because he is on his lunch break.
5. No, she won't.

Common Mistakes

1. cellphone / mobile phone
2. send text messages
3. wake-up call
4. (repair) shop
5. a

Unit 08

Vocabulary

Ⓐ 1. résumé   2. full-time job   3. summer job
4. Bachelor's Degree(BA or BS)
5. Master's Degree(MA, MS, or MBA)
6. PhD/doctorate   7. reference

Ⓑ 1. ⓕ   2. ⓖ   3. ⓐ   4. ⓒ   5. ⓓ   6. ⓘ   7. ⓙ   8. ⓚ
9. ⓔ   10. ⓑ   11. ⓗ   12. ⓝ   13. ⓛ   14. ⓜ

Listening Activity

Ⓐ 1. ⓑ   2. ⓑ   3. ⓒ

Ⓑ experience, reference, team, references, job, matches

Common Mistakes

1. part-time job   2. office worker or businessperson
3. (older) friends[classmates, colleagues, co-workers]
4. open   5. went abroad   6. staff
7. white out, glue, stapler

Unit 09

Starter

Ⓐ 1. burrito   2. pizza   3. hamburger   4. sushi

Vocabulary

Ⓑ 1. seaweed   2. peppers   3. egg   4. bean sprouts
5. tofu   6. garlic

Listening Activity

Ⓐ

	Dave		Lisa	
	Suggests	Reason	Agrees/Disagrees	Reason
❶	Crab cakes	hungry	Disagrees	More expensive
❷	Chicken wings	less expensive, very tasty	Disagrees	Greasy

Ⓑ
1. Curry
2. Too spicy.
3. Because he needs something tastier and more filling.
4. Chinese food
5. Too salty.

Common Mistakes

1. drink   2. throw up, vomit, get sick   3. free
4. supermarket or grocery store   5. a lot   6. Sprite/7-Up
7. omelet with rice   8. cook   9. Bottoms up!

Unit 10

Vocabulary

Ⓐ a. 6   b. 14   c. 2   d. 18   e. 20   f. 15   g. 19
h. 4   i. 13   j. 8   k. 10   l. 17   m. 5   n. 7
o. 11   p. 12   q. 9   r. 3   s. 1   t. 16

Ⓒ 1. They   2. It   3. That's   4. Those are

Grammar Points

1. one   2. one   3. it

Listening Activity

A hat, hat, jacket, one, leather, hat, $45

B 1. A new dress 2. A new one
3. No, she plans to go to the boutiques downtown.
4. No, he doesn't want to go shopping with her.
5. Her sister

Common Mistakes

1. (business/dress) shirt
2. two-piece dress ('two-piece' = bikini!)
3. underwear
4. dress
5. shorts
6. brand name
7. track suit, exercise clothes or gym clothes
8. turtleneck (shirt/sweater)
9. puts on
10. green

Unit 11

Starter

A 1. sunny / clear 2. cloudy 3. snowy 4. rainy

Vocabulary

A 1. Celsius, Fahrenheit 2. clear 3. humid/muggy
4. temperature 5. rainy/monsoon season
6. forecast/report 7. cloudy/overcast

Activity

B 1. 80°F 2. 40°F 3. 34°F

Listening Activity

A 1. From Maine to the Carolinas
2. New Orleans 3. California
4. Arizona 5. New York

B icy, overnight, melt, drop, icing, stick, increase, expected, sunny, temperatures

Common Mistakes

1. blue
2. air-conditioner
3. go on a trip / travel
4. It will rain
5. go skiing
6. snowboard

Writing Activity

1. cloudy, chance, rain, highs, lows
2. sunny, chance, evening, clouds, rain
3. temperatures, freezing, snow, high, low
4. scorcher, high, low, degrees, wind, Hurricane

Unit 12

Starter

B 1. Do you like sports?
2. What kind of sports do you like the most?
3. Which do you prefer, to play sports or to watch sports?
4. Are you good at any sports?

Pair work

A. 2 — 1 — 4 — 3
B. 4 — 2 — 1 — 3
C. 3 — 6 — 1 — 4 — 5 — 2

Listening Activity

	Sport	Opinion	How often
① Sam	workout	love it	every morning
② Nate	golf	hate it	once or twice a year
③ Noah	taekwondo	like it	2-3 times a week

Common Mistakes

1. to swim / swimming 2. bowl
3. to ski / skiing 4. hurts
5. to exercise / exercising
6. to rollerblade / rollerblading

Appendix **125**

This page should be copied four times.